Collins

11+
Verbal
Reasoning

Support & Practice
Workbook

Gemma Taylor and Chris Pearse

Published by Collins
An imprint of HarperCollins*Publishers* Ltd
1 London Bridge Street
London SE1 9GF

HarperCollins*Publishers*
Macken House
39/40 Mayor Street Upper
Dublin 1
D01 C9W8
Ireland

ISBN 978-0-00-856257-1

First published 2023

10 9 8 7 6 5 4 3 2 1

British Library Cataloguing in Publication Data.
A CIP record of this book is available from the British Library.

Publisher: Clare Souza
Authors: Gemma Taylor and Chris Pearse
Project Management: Richard Toms and Tracey Cowell
Cover Design: Kevin Robbins and Sarah Duxbury
Inside Concept Design, Typesetting and Artwork: Ian Wrigley
Production: Emma Wood

Published in collaboration with Teachitright.
Billy the Bookworm™ is the property of Teachitright Ltd.

Printed and bound in the UK using 100% Renewable Electricity at CPI Group (UK) Ltd

Contents

Introduction

Teachitright

This book has been published in collaboration with Teachitright, one of the most successful 11+ tuition companies in the South-East. Teachitright has supported thousands of children for both grammar school and independent school entry. It has several tuition centres across the UK, including Berkshire, Buckinghamshire, Surrey and the West Midlands.

With considerable experience and knowledge, Teachitright has produced a range of books to support children through their 11+ journey for GL Assessment, CEM and many Common Entrance exams. The books have been written by qualified teachers, tested in the classroom with pupils, and adapted to ensure children are fully prepared and able to perform to the best of their ability.

Teachitright's unique mascot, Billy the Bookworm, helps to guide children through this book and gives helpful hints and tips along the way. We hope your child finds this book useful and informative and we wish them luck on their 11+ journey.

Teachitright holds a number of comprehensive revision courses and mock exams throughout the year. For more information, visit **www.teachitright.com**

Helping to build your child's future

GL Assessment Question Types

This book contains different verbal reasoning question types to help your child become familiar with the expectations in the GL Assessment 11+ examination.

These include:

Section 1: Word questions

Section 2: Numeracy

Section 3: Coding questions

Teachitright believes that learning the main strategies and techniques involved will help to develop confidence and ensure that children are fully prepared for the 11+ test.

The book is structured into three key areas:

Learn: In the introduction to each lesson, there is a detailed description of the question type and a worked example. This section also provides tips and hints on how to solve the individual question type.

Develop: This section contains 10 questions to help children understand the format and start applying strategies and techniques acquired in the Learn section.

Succeed: Each lesson ends with a set of questions to try under timed conditions and enables children to apply exam techniques taught throughout the lessons.

This book provides 18 lessons and these can be followed in order or in isolation. It is important to study the Learn sections to ensure the correct techniques are applied when attempting the questions in the Develop or Succeed sections.

Billy the Bookworm provides supportive statements throughout the book to aid understanding.

There is a **marking chart** and **progress grid** at the back of the book to help track your child's development throughout the topics and highlight strengths and weaknesses.

Online Video Tutorial

An online video tutorial to help with techniques is available at
www.collins.co.uk/11plusresources

SECTION I:

WORD

Look out for Billy's tips and hints.

Lesson 1: Closest in Meaning

LEARN

This question type requires a good understanding of synonyms (words with a similar meaning). A thesaurus enables you to look up synonyms quickly and is a useful tool whilst you practise this question type until you are more familiar with the vocabulary.

In these questions you have to find the two words, one from each group, that are the closest in meaning.

Let's look at an example.

Choose two words, one word from each group, which are the most similar in meaning.

(colander considerate thoughtful)   (carefree strain pensive)

Technique

1. You are looking for two words that mean the same, one from each bracket. If you immediately see the two that are closest in meaning, record your answer.

2. If you are not certain you have found two words with the same meaning, you need to work through the words in turn. Use the first word from the first group and check it against each word in the second. Are any of those close in meaning?

   colander and carefree   *colander and strain*   *colander and pensive*

3. If you have not yet found the closest pair, you must repeat the process by pairing the second word from the first group with each word in the second. Are any of those close in meaning?

   considerate and carefree   *considerate and strain*   *considerate and pensive*

4. If your answer is still no, repeat the process again with the third and final word in your first group.

   thoughtful and carefree   *thoughtful and strain*   *thoughtful and pensive*

   The two words with a similar meaning are **thoughtful** and **pensive**.

5. Once you have decided which words are the closest in meaning, double check by substituting one for another in a sentence. Does the sentence still make sense?

   For example:

   The man was thoughtful for a moment before he shrugged casually.

   The man was pensive for a moment before he shrugged casually.

DEVELOP

Choose two words, one word from each group, which are the most similar in meaning.

① (arid artefact ancient) (modern antique dusty)

② (casual loose tense) (relaxed formal asleep)

③ (podium champion second) (winner loser trophy)

④ (cruel ordinary kind) (hero villain mean)

⑤ (flower mild fragrance) (scent sent exotic)

⑥ (destroy create left) (craft wreck war)

⑦ (laugh courteous rude) (impolite mock manage)

⑧ (hit dodge swipe) (swerve blockade crash)

⑨ (confident joke funny) (serious amusing bashful)

⑩ (explain confuse clarify) (shrug summary baffle)

These questions may contain a pair of words with opposite meanings (antonyms) to try to confuse you.

SUCCEED

08:00
8 minutes

Choose two words, one word from each group, which are the most similar in meaning.

① (constitution liberty imprisoned)   (impoverished enslaved freedom)

② (fall rise climb)   (journey ascent peak)

③ (multiple thin meagre)   (generous paltry hungry)

④ (adversary friend argue)   (foe war peace)

⑤ (strengthen relent mild)   (yield severe cease)

⑥ (progress pause digress)   (space return headway)

⑦ (steady busy motion)   (tranquil quiet movement)

⑧ (felicitous threatening innocent)   (ominous rosy favourable)

⑨ (tease laugh humour)   (cry mock reward)

⑩ (fail stagnant thrive)   (flourish dark stunt)

⑪ (lacking grow plentiful)   (abundant minimal destroy)

⑫ (still moving deceased)   (motionless sparkling dizzy)

⑬ (punish heed order)   (monarch disobey obey)

⑭ (stationary squirm submit)   (wiggle rotate squeak)

⑮ (pamper relax mistreat)   (gluttony indulge comfort)

(16) (advance battle retreat) (stumble rethink withdraw)

(17) (solitary miscellaneous expected) (various gathered connected)

(18) (strengthen muscles weaken) (rebuild regret fortify)

(19) (return poach mischievous) (steal generous beg)

(20) (obvious oblivious vain) (harmonious ignorant attentive)

(21) (patient urgent decisive) (crucial criticise despair)

(22) (tepid scolding burn) (cold kettle lukewarm)

(23) (uninformed equal unanimous) (vote alone united)

(24) (wrench share toolbox) (lift pull carry)

(25) (bustling claustrophobic uninhabited) (deserted loud hot)

(26) (strong frail old) (lift feeble helpless)

(27) (insignificant write trace) (detect ignore monitor)

(28) (promote surpass fail) (lessen survive exceed)

(29) (peel shake enthusiasm) (negativity zest motivated)

(30) (melancholy jolly active) (spirited loud quiet)

BILLY'S PUZZLE PAGE

Synonyms crossword

Can you work out the missing words to complete this crossword from the clues provided?

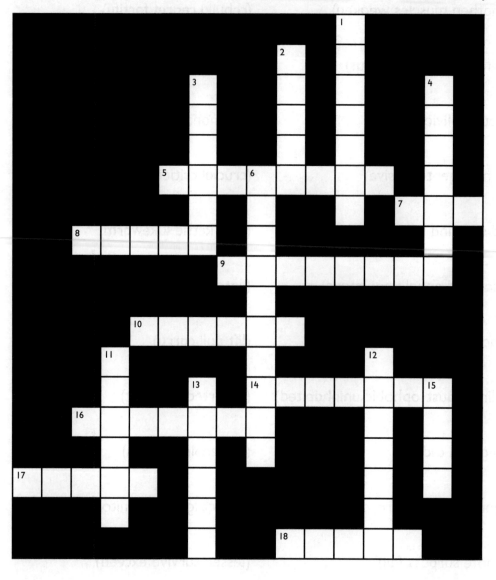

Across

5. A synonym for BLOCK
7. A synonym for CONSUME
8. A synonym for BRIGHT
9. A synonym for YOUNG
10. A synonym for SUDDEN
14. A synonym for TORMENT
16. A synonym for WORRY
17. A synonym for TILT
18. A synonym for WIDE

Down

1. A synonym for HUG
2. A synonym for STYLE
3. A synonym for BAN
4. A synonym for BRAVERY
6. A synonym for VICTORIOUS
11. A synonym for REMIND
12. A synonym for PROBLEM
13. A synonym for HATE
15. A synonym for THROW

LEARN

In this question type, you have to find the pair of words that are opposite in meaning – otherwise known as antonyms.

Let's look at an example.

Choose two words, one word from each group, which are the most opposite in meaning.

(nonsense gift absence)   (presence absent missing)

Technique

1. Read through all of the words in both sets of brackets. Even if you spot the pair of words immediately, continue to check the other words to make sure that you have found two words that are opposites.

2. If you cannot spot the opposites straight away, you will need to work through all of the words in turn until a pair can be found. To do this, select the first word in the first bracket and compare it to each word in the second bracket. Are they opposites?

nonsense and presence   *nonsense and absent*   *nonsense and missing*

3. If the first word from the first bracket is not opposite to any of the words in the second, then it is not a part of the answer. You must now pair the second word from the first bracket with each of the words in the second bracket. Are any of these opposites?

gift and presence   *gift and absent*   *gift and missing*

4. If you have still not found the pair of antonyms or opposites, try the final word in the first bracket with each word in the second bracket. One of these must be the opposite.

absence and presence   absence and absent   absence and missing

The two words that are opposite in meaning are **absence** and **presence**.

A word that is close in meaning is often included to confuse you. Remember, you are looking for opposites.

DEVELOP

Choose two words, one word from each group, which are the most opposite in meaning.

①   (advance transmit greet)   (progress retreat circulate)

②   (unusual drab alluring)   (colourless dark bright)

③   (enemy foe comrade)   (rival colleague ally)

④   (seep flow roll)   (course ebb glide)

⑤   (freedom choice tranquillity)   (liberty peace captivity)

⑥   (lumbering sturdy quick)   (strong feeble clumsy)

⑦   (happy calm hopeful)   (miser content miserable)

⑧   (legendary celebrity obscure)   (unknowable mysterious famous)

⑨   (slow quick nimble)   (steady rapid awkward)

⑩   (obnoxious sincere foolish)   (obstinate wise silly)

SUCCEED

8 minutes

Choose two words, one word from each group, which are the most opposite in meaning.

① (race dawdle amble)   (quick hasten cease)

② (weak bold flexible)   (durable emaciated confident)

③ (develop transmute expand)   (grow contract transform)

④ (suspicious gentle valiant)   (surly shy kind)

⑤ (frequent rare ongoing)   (regular seldom repeatedly)

⑥ (relief sorrow distress)   (joy anger pity)

⑦ (collect sort categorise)   (scatter collate group)

⑧ (average merit succeed)   (accomplish pass fail)

⑨ (serious foolish negligible)   (nonsense trivial stern)

⑩ (disentangle impart unleash)   (emancipate escape imprison)

⑪ (healthy ill germs)   (clean diseased vaccine)

⑫ (bold limited bountiful)   (brave empty boundless)

⑬ (optimist negative prime)   (pessimist hopeful ornithologist)

⑭ (bustling calm contented)   (turbulent soothing tranquil)

⑮ (cross lazy lenient)   (lax strict agile)

16   (voluntary audience mandate)   (optional compulsory tribute)

17   (rising noon dusk)   (sunset twilight dawn)

18   (abundant scattered loathsome)   (plentiful scarce loaded)

19   (malevolent brave candid)   (courageous dastardly cowardly)

20   (flexible debilitated worried)   (strong weak whining)

21   (pantry basement attic)   (roof cellar porch)

22   (reverence despair faith)   (hope misery desolation)

23   (scaffold build structure)   (stack create destroy)

24   (humble whisper wicked)   (modest proud enslaved)

25   (aghast ajar afar)   (open peak closed)

26   (sow seed water)   (plant reap cow)

27   (net sheer opaque)   (blocked translucent transparent)

28   (vacant conspicuous rent)   (spacious occupied empty)

29   (excellence fight virtue)   (vice victory good)

30   (wax clean wick)   (increase candle wane)

BILLY'S PUZZLE PAGE

Find the antonym apples

Billy is on the hunt for juicy red apples! Colour the apples which contain antonyms red. If the apples contain synonyms, colour them green.

Which apples will Billy eat?

dishevelled
tidy

diminutive
petite

cleave
carve

acquired
obtained

feasible
impractical

dwindle
increase

bland
spicy

cynical
trusting

abominable
unpleasant

sob
bawl

intrepid
dauntless

perilous
hazardous

differentiate
combine

radiant
vivid

erratic
consistent

amplify
decrease

Lesson 3: Create a Compound Word

LEARN

When two separate words are merged, they create a compound word – usually a word with an entirely new meaning.

For example:

The word *bookworm* is made from the two words *book* and *worm*.

The two words *blue* and *print* make the compound word *blueprint*.

To complete these questions, you need to find two words that when put together create one correctly spelt word.

Let's look at an example.

Find two words, one from each group, that together make one correctly spelt word. You must not change the order of the letters, and the word from the first group must always go first.

(ball table data)   (bat base basket)

Technique

1. Read through all of the words in both sets of brackets. Can you spot the answer immediately? If you can, record the answer quickly and move on to the next question.

2. If the answer isn't obvious, take the first word in the first bracket and combine it with the first word in the second bracket.

   ball + bat   Is this a compound word? No.

3. Now try to pair the first word from the first bracket with the second word in the second bracket. If you still have not found a compound word, try to combine the first word from the first bracket with the final word in the second bracket.

   ball + base

   ball + basket   Neither of these are compound words.

4. Continue this method of combining one word from the first bracket with one word from the second bracket to check all of the options.

   The answer to this question is **data + base**, which merge to become **database**.

DEVELOP

Find two words, one from each group, that together make one correctly spelt word. You must not change the order of the letters, and the word from the first group must always go first.

①   (all day over)   (brake bored break)

②   (book queen sink)   (king let token)

③   (earn good clock)   (wise nest news)

④   (same be by)   (came ten hive)

⑤   (at up back)   (lass fire stares)

⑥   (air at a)   (line whole plain)

⑦   (doll cup flaw)   (board saucer led)

⑧   (brain vie great)   (tall stem surgery)

⑨   (for fore deep)   (sea sore cast)

⑩   (hedge war all)   (hog maze most)

> **The sounds of the separate words sometimes change when they combine to make a compound word. For example, sea + son merge to become season. Writing the whole word out or saying the word aloud can help you to recognise the answer.**

SUCCEED

 08:00 8 minutes

Find two words, one from each group, that together make one correctly spelt word. You must not change the order of the letters, and the word from the first group must always go first.

①   (for in some)   (get hand front)

②   (wreck copy fast)   (less right break)

③   (see tree grand)   (son more acre)

④   (card cross stone)   (shark did board)

⑤   (dead pierce head)   (end ache ear)

⑥   (care ear in)   (ring case rake)

⑦   (for plaster more)   (bid cast head)

⑧   (book sink queen)   (case king cover)

⑨   (for jig good)   (see saw band)

⑩   (black pencil key)   (stroke whole bored)

⑪   (all mean new)   (while girl agent)

⑫   (life sure ladies)   (timed foot like)

⑬   (four pay reign)   (boots day saw)

⑭   (new by in)   (found print view)

⑮   (tooth head set)   (out back led)

⑯ (many six my)   (fold tie team)

⑰ (back son to)   (knight day let)

⑱ (under sweet over)   (current wait where)

⑲ (four tar so)   (row get die)

⑳ (sport hare table)   (wear trick cloth)

㉑ (slow up no)   (beat stares write)

㉒ (in cell under)   (garment over thyme)

㉓ (wash hang stir)   (up shin stand)

㉔ (sun tea cheque)   (glass mate pot)

㉕ (super bitter be)   (suite impose hive)

㉖ (new bake pay)   (roll in where)

㉗ (food waist wedding)   (band truck bin)

㉘ (gym free time)   (bag stop style)

㉙ (up over back)   (thrust stares route)

㉚ (with drawer bake)   (fall out inn)

BILLY'S PUZZLE PAGE

ABC compound words

Fill in each blank space with a word to make a compound word. You may need to use a dictionary if you cannot think of a suitable word to add. The first one has been done for you

A	along	+	side	=	alongside
B	back	+	_____	=	_____
C	counter	+	_____	=	_____
D	day	+	_____	=	_____
E	earth	+	_____	=	_____
F	fire	+	_____	=	_____
G	good	+	_____	=	_____
H	hand	+	_____	=	_____
I	in	+	_____	=	_____
J	jelly	+	_____	=	_____
K	key	+	_____	=	_____
L	law	+	_____	=	_____
M	moon	+	_____	=	_____
N	nut	+	_____	=	_____
O	over	+	_____	=	_____
P	play	+	_____	=	_____
Q	quick	+	_____	=	_____
R	rain	+	_____	=	_____
S	ship	+	_____	=	_____
T	team	+	_____	=	_____
U	under	+	_____	=	_____
V	volley	+	_____	=	_____
W	watch	+	_____	=	_____
X	*There are no compound words that begin with the letter x.*				
Y	your	+	_____	=	_____
Z	zoo	+	_____	=	_____

LEARN

This question type requires a good understanding of spelling and vocabulary. You need to find one letter that when added to two groups of letters makes four correctly spelt words.

Let's look at an example.

Find the letter that will finish the first word and start the second word of each pair. The same letter must be used for both brackets.

nec (?) night   sin (?) nead

Technique

1. Look at all the letter groups. If you can spot the missing letter from the first word, check that the other three words make sense as well.

2. If the answer is not obvious, choose the group of letters with the most unusual letter combination and pair it with different letters until you find a combination that works. In this example, there are no letters that can follow 'nec' besides 'k'.

3. Now slot 'k' into the brackets and see if it completes all of the words. You should be checking that four correctly spelt words are created.

nec (k) night   sin (k) nead

neck   knight   sink   knead

These are all real and correctly spelt words, so '**k**' must be the answer.

Sometimes writing each word out separately can help you to check your spelling.

DEVELOP

Find the letter that will finish the first word and start the second word of each pair. The same letter must be used for both brackets.

1.   sa (?) ind   ho (?) ho

2.   min (?) are   san (?) art

3.   scar (?) at   fre (?) el

4.   wors (?) rain   ju (?) ear

5.   boo (?) eep   ran (?) lng

6.   sk (?) ield   war (?) ours

7.   dic (?) nd   lac (?) arn

8.   lea (?) ry   scar (?) rail

9.   hu (?) rind   youn (?) naw

10.   crow (?) appy   know (?) ovel

SUCCEED

08:00
8 minutes

Find the letter that will finish the first word and start the second word of each pair. The same letter must be used for both brackets.

①   churc (?) ate   scorc (?) eed

②   bod (?) very   lam (?) ager

③   close (?) able   tar (?) here

④   clea (?) eat   bor (?) iece

⑤   hoo (?) eal   men (?) ry

⑥   bar (?) ruise   absor (?) elt

⑦   car (?) rey   slur (?) orch

⑧   war (?) ould   wor (?) ice

⑨   wol (?) ind   tur (?) ield

⑩   car (?) rince   usur (?) ride

⑪   hu (?) one   lun (?) ame

⑫   ar (?) edal   swar (?) ight

⑬   reac (?) eart   sig (?) ear

⑭   ree (?) not   wea (?) nee

⑮   kil (?) ight   tur (?) ewt

⑯   fea (?) ead   fo (?) ind

⑰   meta (?) ow   hal (?) east

⑱   los (?) erve   his (?) in

⑲   clas (?) low   ha (?) earch

⑳   car (?) orn   ten (?) ime

㉑   fo (?) rid   co (?) rief

㉒   chor (?) ast   sal (?) bb

㉓   so (?) ed   endo (?) ield

㉔   fir (?) ate   alar (?) eal

㉕   sa (?) oat   son (?) rade

㉖   pla (?) ield   pa (?) ear

㉗   plan (?) reat   star (?) ight

㉘   tom (?) uy   lam (?) ury

㉙   stra (?) orry   blo (?) eary

㉚   faw (?) ext   scor (?) ine

BILLY'S PUZZLE PAGE

Word snakes

In this activity, the letter which completes one word will start the next. Are you able to figure out all of the missing letters?

Example: han (d) ea (r) eac (h) el (p) lan

I.   sig (?) ew (?) urre (?) ea (?) ilk

2.   eg (?) rat (?) art (?) ur (?) ake

3.   nai (?) ear (?) ex (?) ende (?) oots

4.   foo (?) eacu (?) on (?) rai (?) ever

5.   wreat (?) un (?) ea (?) unne (?) ail

Sometimes working backwards can help. Look at the last group of letters in the snake. Can you spot what word it is supposed to be?

LEARN

For these questions you have to make two new words by moving a letter from one word to another. Both new words must be spelt correctly, and you cannot change the order of the other letters.

Let's look at an example.

Remove one letter from the first word and add it to the second word to make two new words.

> slide   ink

Technique

1. Look at the two words that you have been given. If you can spot the two new words immediately, record your answer and move on to the next question.

2. If the answer is not obvious, look at the first word and remove one letter at a time. Can you spot any new words?

> s   l   i   d   e
>
> lide   s ide   sl de   sli e   slid

3. By doing this, we can see two possibilities: side and slid. Now we have to check which letter, either the 'l' or the 'e', can be used in the second word to make a correctly spelt word.

> ink   *link*   ilnk   inlk   inkl
>
> ink   eink   ienk   inek   inke

4. Now that we have looked at all the options, we can see that the only combination that makes sense is *side* and *link*, so the letter moved was 'l'.

DEVELOP

Remove one letter from the first word and add it to the second word to make two new words.

① blend   tale

② paint   host

③ peace   car

④ scare   bled

⑤ planet   each

⑥ swing   here

⑦ forge   rein

⑧ hover   eats

⑨ estate   clan

⑩ left   oil

Remember that the letter you move can be placed anywhere in the second word. Writing out all the options can make a real difference when you are stuck.

SUCCEED

Remove one letter from the first word and add it to the second word to make two new words.

1. beacon   vent

2. voice   her

3. threat   tanks

4. witch   hair

5. mince   ear

6. munch   pat

7. driver   tout

8. teamed   appal

9. done   well

10. board   ice

11. spine   and

12. stage   poser

13. three   trust

14. gasped   boater

15. twine   crate

(16) thrust   sake

(17) bear   link

(18) filled   party

(19) hooped   shut

(20) bread   root

(21) latches   with

(22) carer   bake

(23) block   rain

(24) leaden   father

(25) greed   son

(26) mister   sand

(27) pitch   hath

(28) string   camp

(29) barged   stager

(30) movie   host

BILLY'S PUZZLE PAGE

Word ladders

Change one letter at a time to make a new word.

Example:

S E A T

B E A T

B O A T

B O L T

B O L D

Look at the first word in the ladder and the last word in the ladder. Which letter will you move from the last word to be in the second word? In the example, the 's' from *seat* is changed to a 'b' to create *beat*.

C A R E

_____

_____

_____

L I M P

H A N D

_____

_____

_____

L E A F

C O M B

_____

_____

_____

H Y P E

R O S E

_____

_____

_____

T I P S

L I M B

_____

_____

_____

M A N E

LEARN

In these questions you are presented with a sentence. In the sentence, the word in capital letters has had three letters next to each other taken out. Using the sentence to give you clues, you need to work out the missing three-letter word and make sure that the sentence makes sense.

Let's look at an example.

Find the three-letter word that completes the word in capital letters and finishes the sentence.

Lucy **ATDED** tuition sessions at the weekend.

Technique

1. Read the sentence and think about what the incomplete word might be. What might Lucy have done at the weekend? It makes sense that she went to tuition sessions, but this doesn't fit with the capital letters we have been given.

2. Consider other ways of saying went that might fit the spelling in capitals. If you think you know the word, check it fits into the sentence.

   Lucy **ATTENDED** tuition sessions at the weekend.

3. Check that the word you have chosen contains a three-letter word by writing it out and eliminating the letters that you were given in the original question.

   ATTENDED

   The three-letter word answer is **TEN**.

DEVELOP

Find the three-letter word that completes the word in capital letters and finishes the sentence.

1. I took some medicine for my **TERLE** headache.

2. We **STED** elephants on the safari.

3. I need to remember to use **CAAL** letters when I write.

4. The inventor had developed a **FASTIC** idea.

5. I reached for a mug out of the **BOARD**.

6. Mum received a beautiful bouquet of **FERS**.

7. I scanned the **CONTS** page for the chapter that I wanted.

8. After the summer, the boy would attend **COLE**.

9. My uncle was in a car **ACCIT** and broke his leg.

10. Dad was **SCING** when I was late to meet him.

SUCCEED

Find the three-letter word that completes the word in capital letters and finishes the sentence.

① The race would **ST** when we heard the whistle.

② She demonstrated her **KNOWGE** of computers.

③ Everyone **GATED** after the funeral.

④ My grandfather **MANUFURES** toy cars.

⑤ The curry contained **COUT** milk.

⑥ I had **FORTEN** my lines in the school performance.

⑦ The man's baking **INESS** was a roaring success.

⑧ **CAR** cake is usually topped with cream cheese frosting.

⑨ The skyscraper had a **HELITER** pad on the roof.

⑩ The girl was more than **ABLE** of completing her homework independently.

⑪ The bride still needed something **BORED** for the ceremony.

⑫ The **VOY** took longer than the sailor had anticipated.

⑬ Hercules was a **LEGARY** warrior.

⑭ The animal kept **CING** at its cage.

⑮ The ground had **HARED** because it hadn't rained for so long.

(16) The chef would **SPRLE** salt and pepper on the food before sending it out.

(17) My nan wore a **HING** aid as she got older.

(18) He **WED** the potatoes before he peeled them.

(19) Finishing first was a **TREDOUS** result for the new driver.

(20) The children **PRETED** to be pirates in the garden.

(21) My dad makes a **SCPTIOUS** lamb kleftiko.

(22) A **TAGON** is a five-sided shape.

(23) The witness **ACCURLY** described the robber to the police.

(24) The teacher became **IRRITD** when I didn't hand in my homework on time.

(25) My head **THBED** after I banged it.

(26) The priest lit a **CLE** to begin the service.

(27) The thief artfully **ESED** his prison cell.

(28) The **AMPHIATRE** was filled with people.

(29) He bid his friend **EWELL** and he set off on a new adventure.

(30) It was **FORDEN** to enter the forest after dark.

BILLY'S PUZZLE PAGE

Three-letter challenge

Grab a friend or family member and set yourself a timer for three minutes for each board.

Who can make the most three-letter words using only the letters in the board?

Board 1

M	S	E	F
R	A	T	D
L	O	N	E
K	A	F	B

Board 2

A	T	E	M
Y	O	N	I
D	S	V	L
K	P	R	G

Lesson 7: Complete the Third Pair the Same Way

LEARN

In these questions you are given three pairs of words. The first two pairs reveal a pattern that must be used to complete the third pair.

Let's look at an example.

Find the word that completes the third pair of words so that it follows the same pattern as the first two pairs.

    kite   kit   tape   tap   fire _____

Technique

1. Look at the first pair of words. How does the second word differ from the first?

    kite   kit   The second word has dropped the 'e'.

2. Now check this rule against the second pair. Does the rule apply to this pair too?

    tape   tap   The 'e' has been dropped again.

3. Apply the rule to the third pair to find the missing word.

    fire   fir   The answer is **fir**.

Common rules that appear

Common rules include:
- rearranging the letters in the first word to create the second word
- replacing a certain letter with another letter
- removing a letter
- changing a letter for the next one along in the alphabet.

Sometimes the rule is difficult to spot. It can be useful to number the letters to see what has been changed.

Let's look at another example.

Find the word that completes the third pair of words so that it follows the same pattern as the first two pairs.

house   same   moonlight   name   winter   _____

Technique

1. Number the letters in the first word.

h	o	u	s	e
1	2	3	4	5

2. Now look at what letters have been used in the second word. In this example, the fourth letter in the first word has been used to start the second word.

s	a	m	e
4			

3. When you look at the next pair of words, you can see that this pattern has been repeated and that after using the fourth letter, the second word must end in 'ame'.

m	o	o	n	l	i	g	h	t
1	2	3	4	5	6	7	8	9

n	a	m	e
4			

4. Apply this rule to the final word and complete the third pair. Therefore, the answer is **tame**.

Be careful!
Sometimes more than one letter is moved. Occasionally the letters are reordered like a code.

DEVELOP

Find the word that completes the third pair of words so that it follows the same pattern as the first two pairs.

1. pipe   pip   mane   man   song   _____

2. hind   hand   time   tame   wisp   _____

3. beard   ear   hoard   oar   tales   _____

4. shout   shot   solder   sole   fluted   _____

5. mammoth   ham   million   nil   matador   _____

6. emit   time   keep   peek   rats   _____

7. teams   seam   fails   sail   lands   _____

8. bloat   coat   cling   ding   shout   _____

9. start   tart   tripe   ripe   place   _____

10. hinder   rind   rented   dent   parted   _____

SUCCEED

Find the word that completes the third pair of words so that it follows the same pattern as the first two pairs.

① cabbages   sage   wandered   dare   focussed   _____

② define   find   posted   step   mother   _____

③ marks   arm   ready   ear   glove   _____

④ flood   good   boast   cast   stale   _____

⑤ bread   read   grain   rain   cloud   _____

⑥ poster   rest   wanted   dent   hasten   _____

⑦ bigot   big   bushy   bus   singe   _____

⑧ extent   ten   places   ape   inform   _____

⑨ many   any   land   and   said   _____

⑩ camera   mace   sentry   nest   casket   _____

⑪ knits   stink   spots   stops   warts   _____

⑫ grown   row   bodes   ode   brawl   _____

⑬ extending   nets   attests   sets   unsold   _____

⑭ mint   tin   bows   sow   hips   _____

⑮ mail   nail   sale   tale   bows   _____

16 crash   dash   flash   gash   shape   _____

17 writer   rite   shandy   hand   tables   _____

18 barmy   bar   alert   ale   cared   _____

19 fact   act   sink   ink   tout   _____

20 ten   net   war   raw   saw   _____

21 ash   sash   lit   slit   lop   _____

22 jump   lump   dire   fire   rail   _____

23 live   evil   star   rats   time   _____

24 fabric   cab   jetsam   met   caters   _____

25 all   ball   ore   pore   ear   _____

26 task   ask   sand   and   shop   _____

27 mobile   lob   barber   ear   ration   _____

28 grind   grid   tramp   trap   beard   _____

29 bile   bite   male   mate   vole   _____

30 custard   card   violent   vent   sailing   _____

BILLY'S PUZZLE PAGE

Words within a word

These questions test your ability to find patterns and create words using the letters of another word.

Here is an example.

ENGLAND

aged	age	and	an	angel	angled
dale	dangle	deal	den	end	lend

Challenge a friend or a family member – who can find the most words within these words?

MERMAID

WORRIED

SATURN

PARKING

PEDESTRIAN

LEARN

For these questions you have to make a new word from the letters of two other words. You are always given an example; you must figure out how the word in brackets has been formed so that you can apply that rule to the other set of words.

Let's look at an example.

In this question, the three words on the right should go together in the same way as the three words on the left. Work out the missing word and write it in the gap.

    area (read) dent   :   crop (_____) edge

Technique

1. Look at the words on the left. Try to work out how the word in brackets was formed.

   In this question, the 'rea' has been selected from the end of *area* and has been joined with the 'd' from the beginning of *dent*.

   area (read) dent

2. Now use this rule to find the missing word from the right. Take the last three letters of *crop* and the first letter of *edge*.

   crop (_____) edge

   The word created is **rope**.

DEVELOP

In these questions, the three words on the right should go together in the same way as the three words on the left.

Work out the missing word and write it in the gap.

1. host (stir) iron   :   push (__shin__) inch

2. path (have) veto   :   fall (__lash__) ship

3. ban (and) day   :   gin (__inn__) new

4. grass (asset) teach   :   known (__owner__) ready

5. twin (want) tape   :   thus (__host__) tone

6. rip (tip) fat   :   rug (__tug__) tub

7. keep (deep) wild   :   cold (__fold__) wolf

8. oak (oar) rim   :   fog (__for__) raw

9. tech (cast) fast   :   rent (__nice__) dice

10. rush (rust) talk   :   sale (__salt__) team

SUCCEED

08:00
8 minutes

In these questions, the three words on the right should go together in the same way as the three words on the left. Work out the missing word and write it in the gap.

1.   virus (rusty) unity   :   thank (_____) uncle

2.   cycle (clear) arena   :   shown (_____) error

3.   mate (tip) chip   :   duck (_____) flat

4.   hop (open) end   :   ego (_____) new

5.   sort (tray) yard   :   whom (_____) note

6.   bin (tin) yet   :   bad (_____) gas

7.   cost (stop) open   :   bath (_____) away

8.   nets (sent) time   :   need (_____) soup

9.   live (even) seen   :   reef (_____) sell

10.   jar (art) top   :   won (_____) ear

11.   goal (gold) glad   :   fray (_____) were

12.   bribe (beats) stand   :   flesh (_____) trips

13.   led (den) net   :   mug (_____) now

14.   sap (ape) end   :   ore (_____) die

15.   train (trip) ripe   :   speak (_____) wine

⑯ rice (rich) itch : pink (_____) lick

⑰ hurt (turn) none : news (_____) nice

⑱ fluid (fluff) stuff : grade (_____) stand

⑲ alarm (armed) delay : chair (_____) debut

⑳ fate (test) stay : wife (_____) army

㉑ young (youth) mouth : craft (_____) trash

㉒ mail (like) knee : view (_____) rose

㉓ bond (boss) miss : life (_____) sank

㉔ leer (rein) pain : rush (_____) risk

㉕ heart (earth) hence : plate (_____) rough

㉖ sag (age) egg : fax (_____) era

㉗ treat (react) class : other (_____) image

㉘ moon (mode) debt : cook (_____) mere

㉙ mile (mill) lime : case (_____) kept

㉚ lease (least) meant : sharp (_____) solve

BILLY'S PUZZLE PAGE

Word worms

To complete each word worm, you must fill in the missing letters to create a continuous 'worm' of words.

Each pair of joined words must have only one letter that is different and the remaining letters must be the same and in the same place. No words can be repeated.

Can you complete this special Billy challenge?

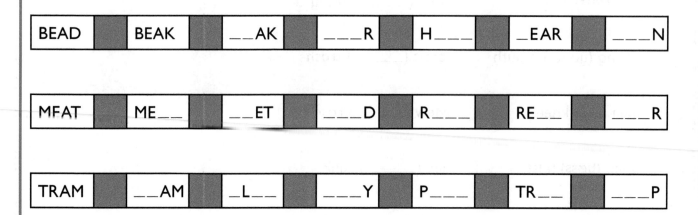

| BEAD | | BEAK | | _ _ AK | | _ _ _ R | | H _ _ _ _ | | _ E AR | | _ _ _ N |

| MFAT | | ME _ _ | | _ _ ET | | _ _ _ D | | R _ _ _ _ | | RE _ _ | | _ _ _ R |

| TRAM | | _ _ AM | | _ L _ _ | | _ _ _ Y | | P _ _ _ _ | | TR _ _ | | _ _ _ P |

LEARN

In these questions you are given a sentence containing a hidden four-letter word. This word is hidden at the end of one word and the beginning of the next. Scanning a sentence quickly and looking for words that start or end with a vowel can help you to locate the hidden four-letter word.

Let's look at an example.

In this sentence, a four-letter word is hidden at the end of one word and the start of the next. Find the pair of words that contains the hidden word.

We saw all of the Harry Potter films at the cinema.

Technique

1. Quickly read through the sentence, scanning the gaps between the words to see if you can spot the hidden four-letter word. If the answer is obvious and you have checked its spelling, record the answer and move on to the next question.

2. If the answer is not obvious, work through the sentence one gap at a time until you spot a four-letter word.

   We saw all of the Harry Potter films at the cinema.

   Each time you do this, you will have to ask yourself if what you have found is a proper word.

   Check these combinations:
   • 1 letter from the end of the first word and 3 letters from the start of the second.
   • 2 letters from the end of the first word and 2 letters from the start of the second.
   • 3 letters from the end of the first word and 1 letter from the start of the second.

3. In this sentence the hidden word is *wall*, but the answer is the pair of words where this word was found. If you look between *saw* and *all* you will see that you had to take 1 letter from the end of the first word and 3 letters from the start of the second.

   The answer is **saw all**.

The hidden four-letter word can be made in many ways, so be thorough in your search.

DEVELOP

In each of these sentences, a four-letter word is hidden at the end of one word and the start of the next. Find and underline the pair of words that contains the hidden word.

1. Each alligator was fed a bucket of fish a day.

2. The new boy ate by himself at lunch.

3. The storm ended by morning.

4. My aunt finally sold her car today.

5. The first arrow found the target.

6. He fell over and scraped his knee.

7. I couldn't see the television from this angle.

8. That wind is bracing.

9. My sister bought her new top at the store.

10. The attack caught them by surprise.

Page 50

SUCCEED

08:00
8 minutes

In each of these sentences, a four-letter word is hidden at the end of one word and the start of the next. Find and underline the pair of words that contains the hidden word.

1. The rooster crowed at dawn.

2. Sam also loved music.

3. There was a lot of risk in this plan.

4. My stomach felt sore inside.

5. An apple costs thirty pence.

6. The cleaners entered the hotel suite.

7. Recycling plastic can help our planet.

8. The little boys hoped for snow.

9. It was the worst open day he had been to.

10. His other daughters were jealous.

11. Nemo damaged his fin during his escape.

12. The fierce enemy thought they had won.

13. A seamstress altered my wedding dress.

14. The police were very confused.

15. His team scored the most points in the league.

(16)   These alleys lead out of the town.

(17)   She called out the register.

(18)   The wren travelled to the closest branch.

(19)   Five invites were delivered by post.

(20)   I couldn't wait for my birthday party.

(21)   The baby grew rapidly in his first few months.

(22)   It was spring one day and suddenly it was summer.

(23)   Appearing in the water was a long ripple.

(24)   Time always flies when you are having fun.

(25)   Mum made them eat their vegetables.

(26)   The woman was granted a completely new identity.

(27)   Dinner consisted of mash and sausages.

(28)   The careless young lad left behind his homework.

(29)   The competitive athlete had a sudden thirst.

(30)   The photographer took the picture quickly.

BILLY'S PUZZLE PAGE

Spell the four-letter words

Each of these triangles contains an assortment of letters. Your challenge is to spell as many four-letter words as you can, using one letter from each row. You may use the letters in any order.

To make it even trickier, perhaps you could set yourself a three-minute timer and play against a family member.

How many words can you make?

Example: **gnat** (each letter is taken from a different line within the triangle)

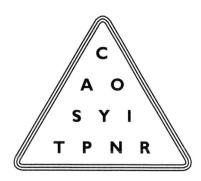

LEARN

This question type is new and requires a good vocabulary. Completing crossword puzzles and experience with wordplay games like Scrabble™ and Boggle™ can help develop anagram-related skills.

In these questions, you must find the letter which has been removed from two words within a sentence. These two words have had their letters rearranged.

Let's look at an example.

This sentence has two words in which the letters have been jumbled up. Rearrange the letters in bold and work out what letter has been removed from both.

At the end of the **WRIABN**, there was a **TP** of gold.

Technique

1. Read the sentence and try to gain an understanding of what it is about. The context should provide you with enough information to guess what the jumbled words might be.

2. A shorter word is usually easier to decipher, since only one letter has been removed. In this question, **TP** is the shorter word and must contain a vowel to make sense, so it is simply a matter of choosing the correct one. A PIT of gold seems unlikely and PAT, TAP, TIP, PUT and PET do not fit into the sentence. A **POT** of gold therefore makes the most sense.

3. Now that you have identified **O** as the letter which has been removed, you must place an **O** amongst the letters of the other jumbled word. This gives you **WRIABNO**.

4. Read the sentence again, focusing on the other jumbled word.

   At the end of the **WRIABNO**, there was a **POT** of gold.

   Is the answer now clear? If it is still not obvious to you, try to look for common letter strings or shorter words within the jumbled word that may help you. The word RAIN can be found and, using all of the letters, the word **RAINBOW** can be made.

   Therefore, the answer is **RAINBOW** and **POT** as the letter **O** was removed from both of the jumbled words.

DEVELOP

These sentences have two words in which the letters have been jumbled up. Rearrange the letters in bold and work out what letter has been removed from both.

1. I prefer to **DRE** a book rather than **CHWT** television.

2. We **DDNEC** underneath the Moon **TTH** night.

3. The **LOFWSE** grew despite the heavy **ANI**.

4. I have to **AWR** my PE kit on **STYUDAS**.

5. In the **WOER**, a princess **SPEL**.

6. You **HEV** to boil water to **KME** tea.

7. A **OL** of people **OUBHG** tickets for the concert.

8. I **WDLU** choose salted popcorn **VRE** sweet.

9. The sign **ISD**: **SYT** off the grass.

10. I never **LYP** football after **KDR**.

SUCCEED

08:00
8 minutes

These sentences have two words in which the letters have been jumbled up. Rearrange the letters in bold and work out what letter has been removed from both.

① I wore my wellies to **MJP** in muddy **PDLESD**.

② We have **IHS** and chips on **RDIYAS** at school.

③ My **AOFUTVRE** flavour of **RSPCS** is cheese and onion.

④ **NECURAM** protects your **IKN** from the sun.

⑤ I watch the **SNW** whilst **TIAGN** my breakfast.

⑥ The **MMAHEDE** lemonade was extremely **RSU**.

⑦ I braided my **ARH** before **OGNG** to bed.

⑧ We **UBIL** a snowman with a **CRARO** for a nose.

⑨ The ice-cream **EGBN** to melt because of the **THE**.

⑩ Four ducklings were **UOFD** inside their **SET**.

⑪ A burglar was **RSTARED** for breaking and **TRINGNE**.

⑫ Apples fell **MFR** the trees in the **CHRDAR**.

⑬ I was **TAE** for **CSOOH** so I had to get the bus.

⑭ My car **BORE** down on the way to **ORW**.

⑮ Rapunzel let down her **AHR** for the prince to **LMCB**.

(16) The **ITER** paced restlessly in its **ACE** at the zoo.

(17) We went ten-pin **OWLIGN** for my **ITHRYDA**.

(18) The teacher expected the **MWOORHK** to be handed in on **ITM**.

(19) A genie **APREEDA** when the **AML** was rubbed.

(20) **UTOSDI** the palace was a beautiful **ARGDN**.

(21) There was a **AP** underneath the princess's **DB**.

(22) The geese were flying **OUSH** for the **INWRE**.

(23) The television **LAEBD** from the other **OMO**.

(24) "**CKP** up your toys before dinner," Dad **ASD**.

(25) Santa knows whether you have been **YAGUHT** or **CIE**.

(26) Spotlights **NHOE** down upon the actor on the **GTAE**.

(27) The **LEIERVY** man left the parcel by the **ORO**.

(28) I bought **WE** glasses after visiting the **POTIIAC**.

(29) The doctor **CESRRIBPD** me some medicine for my **LLNSIS**.

(30) **FORSEWRK** lit up the sky on Bonfire **TNGH**.

BILLY'S PUZZLE PAGE

Anagrams

Complete the anagram of each word by filling in the correct letters.

H O R S E S _ _ R _	H E A R T E _ _ T _	B R E A D _ E _ R _
S M I L E _ _ I _ E	P L A T E P E _ _ _	C R A T E _ _ A _ E

Can you create anagrams of these words?

S T A T E

T H E R E

W E I R D

SECTION 2:

NUMERACY

Look out for Billy's tips and hints.

LEARN

These maths-style questions resemble basic algebra, where letters represent numbers. This question type relies on your knowledge of number bonds, times tables and the four mathematical operations (addition, subtraction, multiplication and division). However, it is not enough to simply find the answer to the sum; you must also record your answer as a letter.

Let's look at an example.

Use the information given, where letters stand for numbers, to answer the sum. Write your answer as a letter.

A = 6   B = 7   C = 3   D = 4   E = 2

(D × C + E) ÷ B = (?)

Technique

1. Write the numerical values beneath the letters to create a sum that you can answer.

    (D × C + E) ÷ B = (?)

    (4 × 3 + 2) ÷ 7 = (?)

2. Work through the sum, using BIDMAS, to reach an answer. If it is a tricky sum with more than one operation, write the answer to each part as you go.

    (D × C + E) ÷ B = (?)

    4 × 3   + 2   ÷ 7 = (?)

    4 × 3 = 12   12 + 2 = 14   14 ÷ 7 = (?)

3. Find the letter that represents your answer. If your answer is not represented by a letter, check through your workings again as the answer will always be one of the given letters.

    14 ÷ 7 = 2   2 = **E**

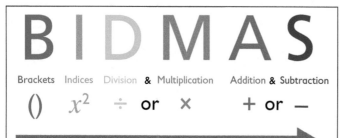

BIDMAS

Brackets	Indices	Division & Multiplication	Addition & Subtraction
()	x^2	÷ or ×	+ or −

ORDER OF OPERATIONS

Remember to do any sums in brackets before you work from left to right through the calculation.

DEVELOP

Use the information given, where letters stand for numbers, to answer the sum. Write your answer as a letter.

①   A = 10   B = 5   C = 4   D = 9   E = 1

     $(A + B) - (D + E) =$

②   A = 12   B = 18   C = 3   D = 10   E = 1

     $A + B \div C =$

③   A = 1   B = 6   C = 10   D = 2   E = 4

     $B^2 \div (C - A) =$

④   A = 2   B = 3   C = 4   D = 8   E = 5

     $A \times B \times C \div D =$

⑤   A = 3   B = 7   C = 5   D = 4   E = 10

     $B \times C \div (D + A) =$

⑥   A = 5   B = 10   C = 20   D = 4   E = 1

     $C \div A + (B - D) =$

⑦   A = 9   B = 3   C = 2   D = 30   E = 12

     $D - (A \times C) =$

⑧   A = 4   B = 3   C = 5   D = 6   E = 7

     $A^2 + B^2 = ?^2$

⑨   A = 14   B = 10   C = 6   D = 5   E = 11

     $(A + B + C) \div D =$

⑩   A = 12   B = 4   C = 20   D = 8   E = 2

     $D \times B - A =$

SUCCEED

15:00
15 minutes

Use the information given, where letters stand for numbers, to answer the sum. Write your answer as a letter.

①   A = 25   B = 13   C = 15   D = 20   E = 3
     B + C – E =

②   A = 42   B = 7   C = 63   D = 54   E = 9
     A ÷ B × E =

③   A = 5   B = 84   C = 4   D = 20   E = 90
     C × D + C =

④   A = 50   B = 20   C = 12   D = 18   E = 21
     D + B + C =

⑤   A = 60   B = 15   C = 50   D = 45   E = 25
     A + B – C =

⑥   A = 10   B = 2   C = 8   D = 40   E = 12
     A ÷ B × C =

⑦   A = 4   B = 1   C = 8   D = 2   E = 12
     D ÷ B × C – A =

⑧   A = 6   B = 24   C = 20   D = 11   E = 19
     D + E – A =

⑨   A = 5   B = 20   C = 4   D = 15   E = 25
     B ÷ C × A – A =

⑩   A = 27   B = 36   C = 9   D = 30   E = 12
     A ÷ C × E =

⑪   A = 45   B = 9   C = 10   D = 35   E = 5
     B × E – C =

⑫   A = 60   B = 8   C = 2   D = 22   E = 5
     A ÷ E + B + C =

⑬   A = 28   B = 44   C = 7   D = 5   E = 11
     B ÷ E × C =

⑭   A = 25   B = 5   C = 4   D = 50   E = 20
     (D – A) × C ÷ B =

(15) A = 10   B = 49   C = 7   D = 70   E = 50
D ÷ A × C =

(16) A = 18   B = 20   C = 40   D = 50   E = 12
(C − A) + (C − E) =

(17) A = 3   B = 4.5   C = 13   D = 11   E = 2
D ÷ E + B + A =

(18) A = 2   B = 4   C = 9   D = 12   E = 8
(B + A) × D ÷ E =

(19) A = 12   B = 8   C = 6   D = 2   E = 5
(B × C) ÷ A − D =

(20) A = 12   B = 3   C = 19   D = 6   E = 13
(B × A) ÷ (C − E) =

(21) A = 4   B = 12   C = 5   D = 3   E = 10
A × C × D ÷ B =

(22) A = 30   B = 80   C = 10   D = 11   E = 12
C × D − A =

(23) A = 72   B = 73   C = 24   D = 3   E = 9
C ÷ D × E =

(24) A = 6   B = 16   C = 4   D = 30   E = 9
B ÷ C × E − A =

(25) A = 14   B = 7   C = 2   D = 20   E = 16
A × C ÷ B + E =

(26) A = 15   B = 12   C = 3   D = 4   E = 48
(B ÷ D) + (A × C) =

(27) A = 14   B = 20   C = 5   D = 21   E = 19
(E + B − A) ÷ C =

(28) A = 4   B = 2   C = 8   D = 16   E = 24
D × B ÷ A =

(29) A = 17   B = 10   C = 13   D = 31   E = 9
B + C + A − E =

(30) A = 4   B = 40   C = 8   D = 12   E = 3
(E × C) + (A × A) =

BILLY'S PUZZLE PAGE

Expensive letters

In this code, each letter represents a money amount.

A	B	C	D	E	F	G	H	I	J	K	L	M
1p	2p	3p	4p	5p	6p	7p	8p	9p	10p	11p	12p	13p

N	O	P	Q	R	S	T	U	V	W	X	Y	Z
14p	15p	16p	17p	18p	19p	20p	21p	22p	23p	24p	25p	26p

Can you find a word that costs exactly 50p?

What is the most expensive word that you can create?

LEARN

In these questions you are asked to find a number to continue a given sequence. First work out the rule and then apply it to complete the number pattern. Look at whether the sequence is ascending (the numbers are getting bigger) or descending (the numbers are getting smaller).

Let's look at an example.

Find the number that continues the sequence in the most logical way.   3   5   7   9   (?)

Technique

1. First, look at the sequence given. Can you spot the rule straight away? If so, note down your answer and move on. As this is a simple sequence, you may have recognised the pattern on sight.

2. If you aren't able to spot the pattern, you must now focus on the difference between each of the numbers and write it down.

3   5   7   9   (?)
  +2   +2   +2

This is an ascending sequence where the numbers increase by 2 each time. Therefore the answer must be **11**.

In the example above, we had to find the next number in a simple sequence with a regular pattern. If you cannot see a pattern, sometimes you need to look at the difference between alternate numbers in a sequence. There may be two patterns at work!

Let's look at another example.

Find the number that continues the sequence in the most logical way.

10   99   20   88   30   77   40   (?)

Technique

1. Can you spot an obvious pattern? If so, write down your answer and move on.

2. If you aren't able to spot the pattern, look at the difference between each number. Does this help? If so, write down your answer and move on.

3. If you are still unable to work out the pattern and it is not clearly ascending or descending in uniform steps, you need to 'leap frog' to see if there are two alternate patterns being used.

       +10   +10   +10
10   99   20   88   30   77   40   (?)
         –11   –11   –11

The first pattern is increasing by 10 and the second pattern is decreasing by 11 so the next number will be **66**.

DEVELOP

Find the number that continues the sequence in the most logical way.

①   240   120   60   30   (?)

②   5   11   17   23   (?)

③   3   4   6   9   13   18   (?)

④   2   21   4   19   6   17   8   (?)

⑤   3   6   12   24   48   (?)

⑥   4   9   16   25   36   (?)

⑦   11   16   26   41   61   (?)

⑧   85   77   69   61   53   (?)

⑨   84   83   81   78   74   (?)

⑩   48   21   45   26   42   31   39   (?)

In these questions, special sequences are often used, such as prime numbers, square, cube and triangle numbers, and the Fibonacci sequence. Try to get familiar with these sequences.

SUCCEED

Find the number that continues the sequence in the most logical way.

1.   32   34   36   38   40   (?)

2.   3   5   6   10   9   15   (?)

3.   36   45   54   63   (?)

4.   81   64   49   36   (?)

5.   71   64   57   50   (?)

6.   5   23   10   21   15   (?)

7.   51   53   50   52   49   (?)

8.   2000   1000   500   250   (?)

9.   2   4   5   7   8   (?)

10.   0   1   1   2   3   5   (?)

11.   16   32   64   128   (?)

12.   27   30   36   45   57   (?)

13.   4   7   11   18   29   (?)

14.   58   5   57   7   55   10   52   (?)

15.   100   50   60   30   400   (?)

(16)   7   14   28   56   112   (?)

(17)   90   83   84   77   78   71   72   (?)

(18)   9   18   29   42   57   (?)

(19)   16   15   20   13   24   11   28   (?)

(20)   1   3   9   27   81   (?)

(21)   13   26   39   52   65   (?)

(22)   88   1   83   2   73   4   (?)

(23)   392   352   312   272   (?)

(24)   256   128   64   32   (?)

(25)   99   100   103   108   115   (?)

(26)   1   3   6   10   15   (?)

(27)   57   55   51   45   37   (?)

(28)   8   8   16   48   (?)

(29)   144   100   64   36   (?)

(30)   2   6   18   54   162   (?)

BILLY'S PUZZLE PAGE

Matching game

Draw lines to match each sequence to its rule.

5 10 15 20		Add 0.5
27 24 21 18		Subtract 9
2 4 8 16		Add 5
1000 100 10 1		Multiply by 2
24 36 48 60		Subtract 3
81 72 63 54		Add 12
2 6 18 54		Divide by 10
100 50 25		Multiply by 3
1 1.5 2 2.5		Divide by 2

Lesson 13: Find the Number to Complete the Sum

LEARN

To answer these 'balanced equation' questions, you need to find the missing number to complete the sum correctly. You have to find the total on one side of the equals sign and work out the missing number to make the same total on the other side.

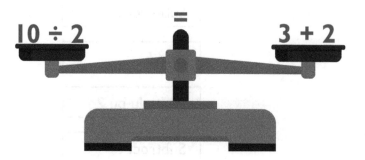

Imagine placing the sum on a pair of scales. Both sides must equal the same and keep the scale balanced!

Let's look at an example.

Find the missing number to complete the sum correctly. $30 \div 5 = 10 - (?)$

Technique

1. Read through the whole question and find the equals sign which separates the two sums.

2. Answer the sum which does not contain a missing number. In this example, that is the calculation on the left.

   $30 \div 5$ $= 10 - (?)$ $30 \div 5 = 6$

   $6 = 10 - (?)$

3. Look carefully at the operation in the remaining sum. Now work out the last calculation. 10 subtract something equals 6. Therefore the missing number must be **4**.

Let's look at another example.

Find the missing number to complete the sum correctly.   14 × 2 − 6 = 9 × 3 + 3 − (?)

Technique

1. Find the equals sign which separates the two sums.

2. Answer the sum which does not contain a missing number. In this example, that is the calculation on the left.

   14 × 2 − 6 = 9 × 3 + 3 − (?)   14 × 2 − 6 = 22

   22 = 9 × 3 + 3 − (?)

3. Look carefully at the operations used in the incomplete calculation. There are three.

   22 = 9 × 3 + 3 − (?)   9 × 3 = 27

   22 = 27 + 3 − (?)   27 + 3 = 30

   22 = 30 − (?)

   30 subtract something is 22. The missing number must be **8**.

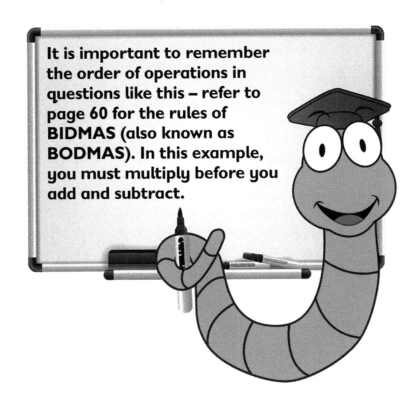

It is important to remember the order of operations in questions like this – refer to page 60 for the rules of **BIDMAS** (also known as **BODMAS**). In this example, you must multiply before you add and subtract.

DEVELOP

Find the missing number to complete the sum correctly.

① $60 \div 12 = 7 - (?)$

② $36 - 9 = 9 \times (?)$

③ $42 \div 6 = 11 - (?)$

④ $8 \times 3 = 10 + (?)$

⑤ $4 \times 4 + 2 = 3 \times (?)$

⑥ $45 \div 3 - 3 = 4 \times (?)$

⑦ $30 \div 6 + 11 = 8 + (?)$

⑧ $20 \div 2 + 5 = 30 \div (?)$

⑨ $7 \times 3 + 9 = 5 \times (?)$

⑩ $48 \div 6 + 2 = 39 - (?)$

SUCCEED

05:00
5 minutes

Find the missing number to complete the sum correctly.

1. $18 \div 2 + 1 = 3 + 17 - (?)$

2. $5 \times 7 - 10 = 50 \div (?)$

3. $6 \times 4 + 10 - 4 = 2 \times (?)$

4. $20 \div 5 \times 10 - 5 = 7 \times (?)$

5. $9 \times 9 - 11 - 10 = 5 \times (?)$

6. $15 \times 2 - 9 = (5 + 2) \times (?)$

7. $10 \times 5 - 28 = (20 - 9) \times (?)$

8. $33 \div 3 + 8 = 3 \times 4 + (?)$

9. $4 \times 3 \times 3 = 5 \times 6 + (?)$

10. $9 + 18 + 3 = 100 \div 4 + (?)$

⑪ $242 - (?) = 99 - 13$

⑫ $419 + 172 = 1000 - (?)$

⑬ $800 - 122 = 86 + (?)$

⑭ $172 - (?) = 59 + 19$

⑮ $672 - (?) = 100 - 56$

⑯ $421 + 1025 = 3000 - (?)$

⑰ $1672 - (?) = 1000 - 99$

⑱ $1765 - 218 = 480 + (?)$

⑲ $1960 - 120 = 835 + (?)$

⑳ $613 + 427 = 1600 - (?)$

Questions 11–20 only contain addition and subtraction because the numbers involved are a lot larger. You will need to use your knowledge of inverse operations to help you find the missing number. Follow the technique you have learned and complete half of the sum before using the inverse to find the missing number.

BILLY'S PUZZLE PAGE

Beat the clock!

This activity can be played with a friend or family member to help you work quickly and develop speedy mental strategies. All that is required is a pen and paper.

- First write a three-digit number at the top of the page.

- Take it in turns to choose five random numbers between 1 and 50. Use these numbers in sums to see how close to the target three-digit number you each can get. You can use any operations (+, −, ×, ÷) but can only use each number once.

- You have three minutes to try to reach the target number.

Right, get playing!

Example:

Target number 134

Random numbers chosen: 6   7   5   10   9

Example of page jottings:

6 + 7 = 13	13 × 10 = 130
9 − 5 = 4	130 + 4 = 134

Increase the challenge

You can vary this game to suit your needs.

Use more random numbers or increase the target number.

Compare methods to see who has used the fewest calculations!

Lesson 14: Find the Missing Number

LEARN

Having a good grasp on your times tables and division facts will help you with this question type. In these questions you are given three sets of numbers; the final set contains a missing number. In order to work out what is missing from the final set, you must work out how the numbers in each set are related to each other.

Let's look at an example.

Find the number that completes the final set of numbers in the same way as the first two sets.

6 (36) 6   5 (25) 5   4 (?) 4

Technique

1. Look at the numbers in the first set. If the number in the middle is the largest of the three, then addition or multiplication must have been used. In this example, 36 is the largest number and is made by multiplying 6 by 6.

2. Now that you have found the rule, check and make sure it works with the second set. It does: 5 × 5 = 25

3. If you are happy that the rule applies to both sets, apply this rule to the final set and find the missing number: 4 × 4 = **16**

Let's look at another example.

Find the number that completes the final set of numbers in the same way as the first two sets.

15 (25) 35   14 (20) 26   12 (?) 48

Technique

1. Look at the numbers in the first set. Since the number in the middle is not the largest, it cannot be a simple addition or multiplication. Check to see if subtraction or division have been used.

2. As no obvious rule can be found, it is time to try multiple operations. In this example, you must add together the two outer numbers and divide by 2 to find the middle number.

3. Check to see if the rule can be applied to the second set. If so, apply this rule to the final set and find the missing number.

12 + 48 = 60

So the missing number is 60 ÷ 2 = **30**

DEVELOP

Find the number that completes the final set of numbers in the same way as the first two sets.

①   20 (80) 60   15 (45) 30   13 (?) 32

②   49 (17) 32   63 (12) 51   99 (?) 45

③   72 (9) 8   44 (4) 11   96 (?) 12

④   13 (39) 3   15 (60) 4   16 (?) 2

⑤   14 (30) 2   9 (40) 4   5 (?) 4

⑥   50 (25) 2   8 (6) 3   11 (?) 8

⑦   36 (11) 25   16 (14) 100   9 (?) 81

⑧   108 (12) 9   69 (23) 3   84 (?) 12

⑨   25 (8) 9   30 (9) 12   50 (?) 16

⑩   17 (72) 19   22 (118) 37   18 (?) 13

If you can't find an obvious rule, it may be because more than one operation is being applied.

SUCCEED

15:00
15 minutes

Find the number that completes the final set of numbers in the same way as the first two sets.

①   6 (7) 42   9 (6) 54   11 (?) 121

②   9 (73) 8   13 (53) 4   12 (?) 4

③   32 (24) 56   45 (48) 93   36 (?) 105

④   20 (49) 29   25 (65) 40   13 (?) 39

⑤   14 (42) 3   9 (90) 10   17 (?) 2

⑥   144 (24) 6   91 (13) 7   108 (?) 9

⑦   13 (19) 25   5 (8) 11   20 (?) 32

⑧   2 (24) 24   3 (24) 16   4 (?) 32

⑨   2 (20) 9   9 (29) 10   4 (?) 18

⑩   69 (107) 38   17 (109) 92   28 (?) 56

⑪   25 (5) 125   8 (20) 160   15 (?) 165

⑫   3 (7) 4   6 (45) 9   5 (?) 10

⑬   13 (52) 4   7 (56) 8   21 (?) 3

⑭   50 (34) 8   72 (60) 6   65 (?) 9

⑮   48 (90) 138   36 (62) 98   59 (?) 87

⑯   6 (52) 4   7 (53) 2   9 (?) 8

⑰   20 (34) 48   16 (33) 50   30 (?) 62

⑱   10 (15) 20   8 (14) 20   28 (?) 42

⑲   11 (154) 14   9 (117) 13   17 (?) 3

⑳   99 (132) 33   120 (167) 47   86 (?) 51

㉑   75 (51) 25   30 (46) 60   20 (?) 46

㉒   88 (22) 4   90 (6) 15   91 (?) 7

㉓   81 (33) 48   73 (37) 36   102 (?) 56

㉔   35 (19) 45   18 (9) 22   14 (?) 46

㉕   11 (48) 13   19 (50) 6   18 (?) 15

㉖   23 (207) 9   16 (80) 5   14 (?) 6

㉗   220 (11) 20   135 (15) 9   156 (?) 12

㉘   50 (64) 7   25 (31) 3   40 (?) 16

㉙   29 (92) 63   58 (107) 49   83 (?) 74

㉚   66 (27) 39   58 (41) 17   94 (?) 65

BILLY'S PUZZLE PAGE

Find the missing number

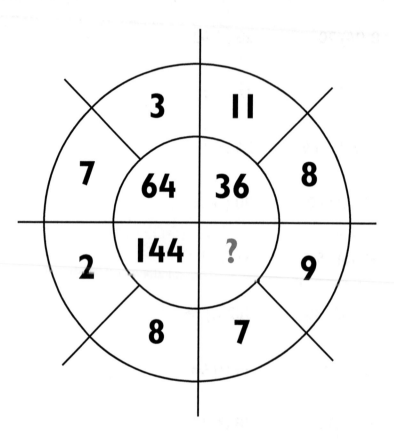

Focus on one quadrant (quarter) at a time.

SECTION 3:

CODES

Look out for Billy's tips and hints.

LEARN

In this type of question, you are given a word and you need to use the alphabet to find out the code. Alternatively, you may be given a code and have to work out the word. A strong grasp of the alphabet and the ability to spot patterns is beneficial when answering these questions.

Let's look at an example.

A B C D E F G H I J K L M N O P Q R S T U V W X Y Z

Use the alphabet to help you with this question.

If the code for **BAKE** is **CBLF**, what is the code for **COOK**?

Technique

1. Consider whether the question wants you to find a word or a code. Codes are a combination of letters, whereas a word will make sense to you. In this example, we are looking for a code.

2. Write the code for the word underneath it, so you can see how the letters have changed. Here, **B** has become **C**, **A** has become **B**, and so on.

    B A K E

    C B L F

3. Now look back at the alphabet and try to spot a pattern between the word and the code. These questions often involve counting forwards or backwards between letters, and you will need to be accurate with your counting if you wish to crack the code. In this example, B becomes C which is a step forward of 1 in the alphabet, and this pattern repeats itself with the subsequent letters (**A** to **B**, **K** to **L**, etc.).

4. Now that you have spotted the pattern for the original word, you can find the code for the second word.

    C O O K +1 step for each letter

    D P P L

    The code for **COOK** is **DPPL**.

Sometimes the step count between letters changes for each letter in the word. Do not assume that if there is a step forward of 1 for the first letter, all the other letters in the word will be the same. Check each letter in turn.

Let's look at another example.

In the previous example, we had to count the steps between the letters in the original word and the letters in the code. Another common question type uses a 'letters partner' or 'mirror code' technique. When counting between the letters does not help crack the code, this is the approach you should try.

A B C D E F G H I J K L M N O P Q R S T U V W X Y Z

Use the alphabet to help you with this question.

If the code for **FEAST** is **UVZHG**, what is the code for **DRINK**?

Technique

1. There are 26 letters in the alphabet. Imagine that a mirror lies between M and N, splitting the alphabet in half. By numbering the alphabet, we are able to see which letters are 'partners', or which ones mirror one another, such as A and Z or M and N.

A	B	C	D	E	F	G	H	I	J	K	L	M	N	O	P	Q	R	S	T	U	V	W	X	Y	Z
1	2	3	4	5	6	7	8	9	10	11	12	13	13	12	11	10	9	8	7	6	5	4	3	2	1

The first letter in **FEAST** is a mirror of the first letter in **UVZHG**.

F and **U** both equal 6, so they are partners.

The last letter in **FEAST** is also a mirror of the last letter in **UVZHG**.

T and **G** both equal 7, so they are also partners.

2. Now that you have established that this is a mirror code question, use the alphabet to work out the code for **DRINK**.

D is 4   **R** is 9   **I** is 9   **N** is 13   **K** is 11

4 = **W**   9 = **I**   9 = **R**   13 = **M**   11 = **P**

So the code is **WIRMP**.

If you check the first and last letter of your word, you are usually able to establish quickly if you are dealing with a mirror code question. By doing this, you will also be able to eliminate many of the answer options.

DEVELOP

A B C D E F G H I J K L M N O P Q R S T U V W X Y Z

Use the alphabet to help you with these questions.

①   If the code for **ENGLISH** is **FOHMJTI**,
what does **NBUIT** mean?

②   If the code for **LISTEN** is **KGPPZH**,
what does **QCPLJHW** mean?

③   If the code for **LIGHT** is **NKIJV**,
what does **FCTM** mean?

④   If the code for **FIRE** is **CFOB**,
what is the code for **WATER**?

⑤   If the code for **CHILD** is **HMNQI**,
what is the code for **ADULT**?

⑥   If the code for **STORY** is **HGLIB**,
what is the code for **NOVEL**?

⑦   If the code for **LOVE** is **OLEV**,
what is the code for **HATE**?

⑧   If the code for **CITY** is **XRGB**,
what is the code for **TOWN**?

⑨   If the code for **CONCERT** is **XLMXVIG**,
what does **KOZB** mean?

⑩   If the code for **DOOR** is **WLLI**,
what does **DRMWLD** mean?

SUCCEED

15:00
15 minutes

A B C D E F G H I J K L M N O P Q R S T U V W X Y Z

Use the alphabet to help you with these questions.

1. If the code for **READ** is **IVZW**,
   what is the code for **WRITE**?

2. If the code for **BOY** is **YLB**,
   what is the code for **GIRL**?

3. If the code for **MEADOW** is **LCXZJQ**,
   what is the code for **FOREST**?

4. If the code for **RICH** is **TMEL**,
   what is the code for **POOR**?

5. If the code for **COFFEE** is **DPGGFF**,
   what does **UFB** mean?

6. If the code for **COUGH** is **DQXKM**,
   what does **TPHIEK** mean?

7. If the code for **SKIP** is **HPRK**,
   what does **QFNK** mean?

8. If the code for **SKIRT** is **HPRIG**,
   what does **HSLIGH** mean?

9. If the code for **SLEEP** is **HOVVK**,
   what is the code for **AWAKE**?

10. If the code for **WIND** is **DRMW**,
    what is the code for **RAIN**?

11. If the code for **CAR** is **XZI**,
    what is the code for **TRAIN**?

12. If the code for **HOPE** is **FMNC**,
    what is the code for **DREAM**?

A B C D E F G H I J K L M N O P Q R S T U V W X Y Z

⑬ If the code for **LEARN** is **MDBQO**,
what is the code for **TEST**?

⑭ If the code for **BEGIN** is **EHJLQ**,
what is the code for **END**?

⑮ If the code for **MOVIE** is **NLERV**,
what does **XRMVNZ** mean?

⑯ If the code for **BROTHER** is **YILGSVI**,
what does **HRHGVI** mean?

⑰ If the code for **FRIEND** is **UIRVMW**,
what does **ULV** mean?

⑱ If the code for **SHOE** is **RGND**,
what does **RNBJ** mean?

⑲ If the code for **FISH** is **KNXM**,
what does **HMNUX** mean?

⑳ If the code for **RED** is **PCB**,
what does **ZJSC** mean?

BILLY'S PUZZLE PAGE

Coded wordsearch

A B C D E F G H I J K L M N O P Q R S T U V W X Y Z

If the code for **PLAY** is **QNDC**,
what are the codes for the following words?

GAME	**CODE**	**ALPHABET**	**LETTERS**	**SEARCH**
WORD	**FUN**	**WIN**	**LOSE**	**CRACK**

Can you find the codes in the wordsearch?

G	T	G	H	P	G	G	I	X	G	M	X	Q	K
L	Q	X	G	V	S	P	M	K	X	W	Z	D	G
K	T	T	G	S	C	G	G	Q	X	G	D	I	G
I	N	T	I	H	V	L	W	X	K	T	X	G	V
L	X	S	M	N	H	V	D	G	T	C	D	Q	N
M	P	P	M	G	S	N	B	B	V	I	H	D	Q
X	M	K	B	N	S	L	F	H	L	B	I	L	Z
C	Q	Q	C	I	F	Z	X	J	X	W	G	M	B
D	V	V	J	P	Z	B	B	W	L	H	H	J	I
M	I	Z	D	G	H	Q	B	M	I	U	P	W	G
V	D	W	W	D	D	H	Q	U	H	Q	W	W	J
G	X	X	W	T	I	Q	Q	W	T	X	W	F	H
W	Z	M	L	D	H	I	G	X	H	D	F	T	D
Q	G	I	Q	L	V	S	V	J	D	U	I	G	Q

Lesson 16: Crack the Number Code

LEARN

For these questions you have to match together numbers and words to crack the code and answer the questions. You will be given four words; three of them will have a code. The codes are not written in the same order as the words, so you must work out which words relate to which codes from the choices available.

Let's look at an example.

The number codes for three of these words are listed in a random order. Work out the code to answer the questions.

BOOK   BOND   BULK   KIND

4532   6114   6704

1. Find the code for **BOND**.

2. Find the code for **LOOK**.

3. Find the word that has the code 6500.

Technique

1. First, try to match together the words and numbers you have been given before attempting the questions underneath. The quickest way to do this is to look for any words with a double letter pattern such as **BOOK**. Since this word contains two Os, its code must contain two of the same numbers in the middle. So the correct code for **BOOK** must be 6114.

   Write the letters beneath the numbers to help you make further matches.

6	1	1	4
B	O	O	K

2. Now that you know the letters for 6, 1 and 4, you can look at the other codes and start to decode them.

4	5	3	2
K	?	?	?

6	7	0	4
B	?	?	K

Whilst there are still some gaps in the codes, you can use your deduction skills to match the remaining words with their codes. Since only one of the words begins with a K, the code 4532 must be **KIND**. Likewise, since we have already found the code for **BOOK**, 6704 must be the code for **BULK**.

4	5	3	2
K	I	N	D

6	7	0	4
B	U	L	K

3. Now that you have matched all the number codes with the correct words, it should be easy to apply your number code to the three questions.

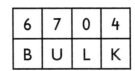

6	I	I	4
B	O	O	K

4	5	3	2
K	I	N	D

6	7	0	4
B	U	L	K

4. Find the code for **BOND**.

Look back at your number codes with the letters underneath. You should now be able to create the code for **BOND** – it is 6132.

5. Find the code for **LOOK**.

Look back at your number codes with the letters underneath. The code for **LOOK** is 0114.

6. Find the word that has the code 6500.

This question simply uses your number codes in reverse. This time, look at the numbers and their corresponding letters to decipher the word – it is **BILL**.

DEVELOP

The number codes for three of these words are listed in a random order. Work out the code to answer the questions.

DAWN   DAYS   YAWN   SAYS

1231   4231   3296

① Find the code for **DAWN**.

② Find the code for **WAYS**.

③ Find the word that has the code 9264.

EASY   TEST   EAST   FAST

8628   5728   6721

④ Find the code for **EASY**.

⑤ Find the code for **FEET**.

⑥ Find the word that has the code 5786.

GOAL   GOLF   FOAL   WOLF

8463   3416   7416

⑦ Find the code for **GOLF**.

⑧ Find the code for **WALL**.

⑨ Find the word that has the code 7161.

If there are no words with a double-letter pattern, look for words containing the same letter twice. For example, in the first question, SAYS starts and ends with the letter S. So the corresponding number code should start and end with the same digit.

SUCCEED

The number codes for three of these words are listed in a random order. Work out the code to answer the questions.

HUNT   HURT   RUNT   HUNG

    2593   6593   6594

①   Find the code for **HURT**.

②   Find the code for **TURN**.

③   Find the word that has the code 2594.

MEET   MEAT   TEAM   MEAL

    2046   2006   2047

④   Find the code for **TEAM**.

⑤   Find the code for **TAME**.

⑥   Find the word that has the code 7420.

KISS   SICK   MISS   MIST

    7516   1539   7511

⑦   Find the code for **KISS**.

⑧   Find the code for **TICK**.

⑨   Find the word that has the code 1957.

PASS   PAST   STEP   PACE

    6954   6933   6931

⑩   Find the code for **STEP**.

⑪   Find the code for **PEST**.

⑫   Find the word that has the code 5931.

REAL   READ   LEAD   RELY

    2465   2468   2481

⑬   Find the code for **LEAD**.

⑭   Find the code for **LEER**.

⑮   Find the word that has the code 6881.

SPOT   SOOT   STOP   SPIT

9221   9361   9321

⑯ Find the code for **STOP**.

⑰ Find the code for **TIPI**.

⑱ Find the word that has the code 1299.

WILL   WIDE   WILD   LIED

5421   7455   7451

⑲ Find the code for **WIDE**.

⑳ Find the code for **WELD**.

㉑ Find the word that has the code 1221.

BILLY'S PUZZLE PAGE

Coded sums

Look carefully at the letters and related numbers in the table. Use this code to help you answer the sums below.

L	O	C	T	G	A	M	B	S	W
5	2	7	3	4	9	6	8	0	1

Example:

LOST + WACG =

5203 + **1974** = 7177

1. BMGO − TSAS =

2. ATGW − BCOS =

3. OGMA + LWLM =

4. ATML + ABTS =

5. BCSG − MBOW =

6. GAOM + LASL =

7. CSWT − TBLG =

8. MGLA + TSMS =

LEARN

In these questions you have to continue and complete a letter series. To do this, you must be confident with the alphabet and be able to spot patterns by counting between letters.

A	B	C	D	E	F	G	H	I	J	K	L	M
1	2	3	4	5	6	7	8	9	10	11	12	13

N	O	P	Q	R	S	T	U	V	W	X	Y	Z
13	12	11	10	9	8	7	6	5	4	3	2	1

Let's look at an example.

A B C D E F G H I J K L M N O P Q R S T U V W X Y Z

Find the pair of letters to continue the series. Refer to the alphabet to help you with this question.

ZG   AI   BK   CM   (?)

Technique

1. First, check for a mirrored pair pattern. If the question contains mirrored pairs, you count the jumps between the pairs, continue the pattern and record the answer.

2. If you can rule out a mirror pattern, as in this example, look carefully at the series for any obvious patterns. Remember, you are looking for a pattern between the first letters in each pair and another between the second letters in each pair.

3. If you can't easily identify a pattern, break down the pairs. Begin by looking at the first letter in each pair. Can you spot a pattern?

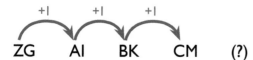

There is a jump of 1 between Z and A, A and B, and B and C. So the next letter will be **D**.

4. Next, look at the second letter in each pair. Can you spot a pattern?

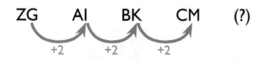

There is a jump of +2 between G and I, I and K, and K and M. So the next letter must be **O**, meaning the missing letter series is **DO**.

DEVELOP

A B C D E F G H I J K L M N O P Q R S T U V W X Y Z

Find the pair of letters to continue the series. Refer to the alphabet to help you with this question.

①	DW	GT	JQ	MN	(?)
②	FS	GS	HT	IT	(?)
③	AA	BZ	DY	GX	(?)
④	TD	SF	RH	QJ	(?)
⑤	ZF	XH	VJ	TL	(?)
⑥	BP	GP	LN	QN	(?)
⑦	CB	DD	EF	FH	(?)
⑧	AZ	BY	CX	DW	(?)
⑨	FM	EN	CO	ZP	(?)
⑩	AB	CD	EF	GH	(?)

Some sequences jump forwards, some jump back and some repeat letters. Adding jump markers to the question and to the alphabet can help you to focus on the pattern.

SUCCEED

A B C D E F G H I J K L M N O P Q R S T U V W X Y Z

Find the pair of letters to continue the series. Refer to the alphabet to help you with this question.

①	ZG	YH	XJ	WK	(?)
②	CX	EV	GT	IR	(?)
③	BI	YI	VJ	SJ	(?)
④	MN	OP	QR	ST	(?)
⑤	FA	HC	GE	IG	(?)
⑥	AC	CE	EG	GI	(?)
⑦	JR	KS	LR	MS	(?)
⑧	XI	ZJ	BL	DO	(?)
⑨	DW	BV	XU	VT	(?)
⑩	WD	TG	QJ	NM	(?)
⑪	TQ	PO	LM	HK	(?)
⑫	ZD	UC	QZ	NY	(?)
⑬	AP	BR	CQ	DS	(?)
⑭	LQ	KR	IT	FW	(?)
⑮	BY	CX	EV	HS	(?)

BILLY'S PUZZLE PAGE

Closest to 50

This game helps you to practise counting between letters. Play it with a friend or a family member.

A B C D E F G H I J K L M N O P Q R S T U V W X Y Z

How to play:

1. Select a word of any length.

    L E T T E R S

2. Count the jumps between each letter (forwards or backwards) and add them together.

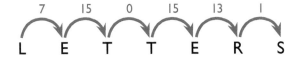

7 + 15 + 0 + 15 + 13 + 1 = 51

3. The person with the total closest to 50 wins!

Remember that double-letter words contain a jump of zero. This could be an advantage or a disadvantage depending on your choice of word!

LEARN

For this question type, you have to find the relationship between pairs of letters to complete a letter sentence. You may need to jump forwards past the letter Z, or backwards from A. It is important that you learn to treat the alphabet as a continuous line.

For instance: A B C D E F G H I J K L M N O P Q R S T U V W X Y Z A B C D E...

Let's look at an example.

Select the pair of letters that completes the sentence in the most sensible way. Use the alphabet to help you.

A B C D E F G H I J K L M N O P Q R S T U V W X Y Z

AZ is to **CY** as **FT** is to (??)

Technique

1. As with other code-style questions, you are looking for one pattern between the first letters of each pair and another pattern between the second letters. So how do we get from **A** to **C**? By looking at the alphabet, we can count the number of jumps.

> More often than not, the pattern between the first letters is different from the pattern between the second letters. **Always check to be sure!**

2. Now that we know there is a forward jump of 2 between the first letters, we can address the third pair and start to work out the unknown letters in the fourth pair. Since **A** to **C** is a forward jump of 2, we must also jump forward 2 from **F**, meaning that the first unknown letter must be **H**.

In our example, the second letters are **Z** and **Y**, which require a jump of −1. If we look at the third pair and its second letter of **T**, a backward jump of 1 means that the second unknown letter must be **S**.

So the pair of letters that completes the number sentence is **HS**.

DEVELOP

Select the pair of letters that completes each sentence in the most sensible way. Use the alphabet to help you.

A B C D E F G H I J K L M N O P Q R S T U V W X Y Z

①	**CG**	is to	**AI**	as	**DN**	is to	(??)
②	**HD**	is to	**KG**	as	**LC**	is to	(??)
③	**TS**	is to	**QT**	as	**SW**	is to	(??)
④	**MA**	is to	**OD**	as	**PG**	is to	(??)
⑤	**RZ**	is to	**SV**	as	**GT**	is to	(??)
⑥	**LU**	is to	**GV**	as	**CW**	is to	(??)
⑦	**FE**	is to	**GG**	as	**ZO**	is to	(??)
⑧	**JQ**	is to	**IO**	as	**SM**	is to	(??)
⑨	**XW**	is to	**AT**	as	**RD**	is to	(??)
⑩	**PK**	is to	**RL**	as	**EZ**	is to	(??)

SUCCEED

15:00
15 minutes

Select the pair of letters that completes each sentence in the most sensible way. Use the alphabet to help you.

A B C D E F G H I J K L M N O P Q R S T U V W X Y Z

① **JM** is to **IS** as **BP** is to (??)

② **WO** is to **UM** as **GL** is to (??)

③ **MG** is to **JI** as **PX** is to (??)

④ **HL** is to **JH** as **DM** is to (??)

⑤ **DH** is to **CI** as **YC** is to (??)

⑥ **AA** is to **XD** as **CB** is to (??)

⑦ **SB** is to **ND** as **JO** is to (??)

⑧ **PX** is to **MZ** as **AE** is to (??)

⑨ **EC** is to **AE** as **MF** is to (??)

⑩ **KF** is to **HI** as **PQ** is to (??)

⑪ **YP** is to **CM** as **FC** is to (??)

⑫ **OQ** is to **PO** as **BR** is to (??)

⑬ **IL** is to **NG** as **SZ** is to (??)

⑭ **FM** is to **DP** as **GW** is to (??)

⑮ **BO** is to **YP** as **KX** is to (??)

BILLY'S PUZZLE PAGE

Alphabet race

In this question type, you may need to jump forwards past the letter Z or jump back from A. Therefore, the alphabet becomes a continuous line of letters. This activity will help you to remember where to go after you reach Z.

- You will need a dice and each player needs a counter. Each player should quickly write out the alphabet in a circle, as below.

- Both players begin on the green letter Z. Each player takes it in turn to roll the dice and count along the alphabet for the number shown on the dice.

- The player who returns exactly to the green Z first is the winner.

THIS PAGE HAS DELIBERATELY BEEN LEFT BLANK

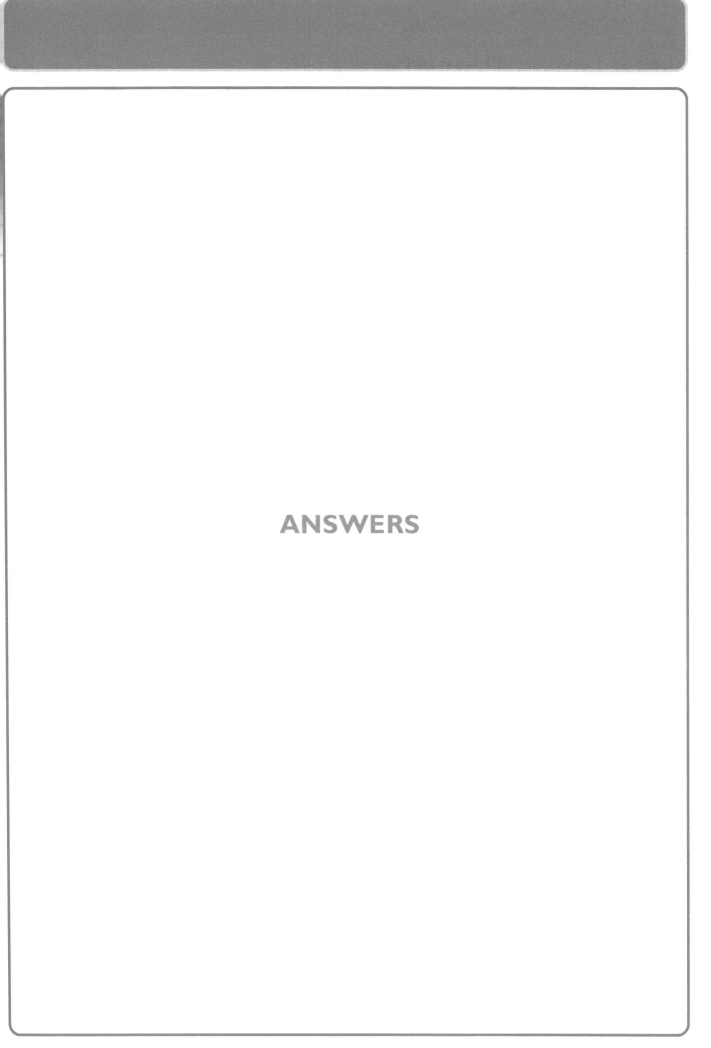

ANSWERS

Lesson 1 answers: Closest in Meaning

Develop: Closest in Meaning (page 9)

1.	(arid artefact **ancient**)	(modern **antique** dusty)
2.	(**casual** loose tense)	(**relaxed** formal asleep)
3.	(podium **champion** second)	(**winner** loser trophy)
4.	(**cruel** ordinary kind)	(hero villain **mean**)
5.	(flower mild **fragrance**)	(**scent** sent exotic)
6.	(**destroy** create left)	(craft **wreck** war)
7.	(laugh courteous **rude**)	(**impolite** mock manage)
8.	(hit **dodge** swipe)	(**swerve** blockade crash)
9.	(confident joke **funny**)	(serious **amusing** bashful)
10.	(explain **confuse** clarify)	(shrug summary **baffle**)

Succeed: Closest in Meaning (pages 10–11)

1.	(constitution **liberty** imprisoned)	(impoverished enslaved **freedom**)
2.	(fall rise **climb**)	(journey **ascent** peak)
3.	(multiple thin **meagre**)	(generous **paltry** hungry)
4.	(**adversary** friend argue)	(**foe** war peace)
5.	(strengthen **relent** mild)	(**yield** severe cease)
6.	(**progress** pause digress)	(space return **headway**)
7.	(steady busy **motion**)	(tranquil quiet **movement**)
8.	(felicitous **threatening** innocent)	(**ominous** rosy favourable)
9.	(**tease** laugh humour)	(cry **mock** reward)
10.	(fail stagnant **thrive**)	(**flourish** dark stunt)
11.	(lacking grow **plentiful**)	(**abundant** minimal destroy)
12.	(**still** moving deceased)	(**motionless** sparkling dizzy)
13.	(punish **heed** order)	(monarch disobey **obey**)
14.	(stationary **squirm** submit)	(**wiggle** rotate squeak)
15.	(**pamper** relax mistreat)	(gluttony **indulge** comfort)
16.	(advance battle **retreat**)	(stumble rethink **withdraw**)
17.	(solitary **miscellaneous** expected)	(**various** gathered connected)

18.	(**strengthen** muscles weaken)	(rebuild regret **fortify**)
19.	(return **poach** mischievous)	(**steal** generous beg)
20.	(obvious **oblivious** vain)	(harmonious **ignorant** attentive)
21.	(patient **urgent** decisive)	(**crucial** criticise despair)
22.	(**tepid** scolding burn)	(cold kettle **lukewarm**)
23.	(uninformed equal **unanimous**)	(vote alone **united**)
24.	(**wrench** share toolbox)	(lift **pull** carry)
25.	(bustling claustrophobic **uninhabited**)	(**deserted** loud hot)
26.	(strong **frail** old)	(lift **feeble** helpless)
27.	(insignificant write **trace**)	(**detect** ignore monitor)
28.	(promote **surpass** fail)	(lessen survive **exceed**)
29.	(peel shake **enthusiasm**)	(negativity **zest** motivated)
30.	(melancholy **jolly** active)	(**spirited** loud quiet)

Billy's Puzzle Page: Synonyms crossword (page 12)

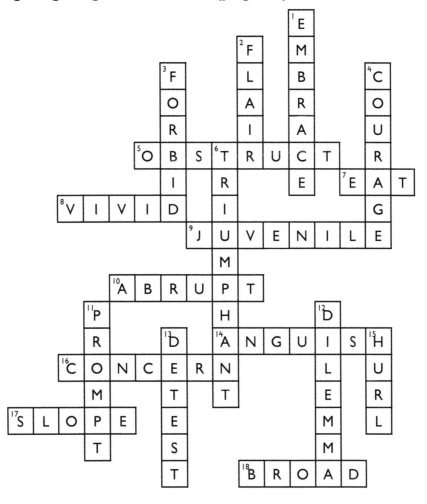

Lesson 2 answers: Opposite in Meaning

Develop: Opposite in Meaning (page 14)

1.	(**advance** transmit greet)	(progress **retreat** circulate)
2.	(unusual **drab** alluring)	(colourless dark **bright**)
3.	(**enemy** foe comrade)	(rival colleague **ally**)
4.	(seep **flow** roll)	(course **ebb** glide)
5.	(**freedom** choice tranquillity)	(liberty peace **captivity**)
6.	(lumbering **sturdy** quick)	(strong **feeble** clumsy)
7.	(**happy** calm hopeful)	(miser content **miserable**)
8.	(legendary celebrity **obscure**)	(unknowable mysterious **famous**)
9.	(**slow** quick nimble)	(steady **rapid** awkward)
10.	(obnoxious sincere **foolish**)	(obstinate **wise** silly)

Succeed: Opposite in Meaning (pages 15–16)

1.	(race **dawdle** amble)	(quick **hasten** cease)
2.	(**weak** bold flexible)	(**durable** emaciated confident)
3.	(develop transmute **expand**)	(grow **contract** transform)
4.	(suspicious **gentle** valiant)	(**surly** shy kind)
5.	(**frequent** rare ongoing)	(regular **seldom** repeatedly)
6.	(relief **sorrow** distress)	(**joy** anger pity)
7.	(**collect** sort categorise)	(**scatter** collate group)
8.	(average merit **succeed**)	(accomplish pass **fail**)
9.	(**serious** foolish negligible)	(nonsense **trivial** stern)
10.	(disentangle impart **unleash**)	(emancipate escape **imprison**)
11.	(**healthy** ill germs)	(clean **diseased** vaccine)
12.	(bold **limited** bountiful)	(brave empty **boundless**)
13.	(**optimist** negative prime)	(**pessimist** hopeful ornithologist)
14.	(bustling **calm** contented)	(**turbulent** soothing tranquil)
15.	(cross lazy **lenient**)	(lax **strict** agile)
16.	(**voluntary** audience mandate)	(optional **compulsory** tribute)
17.	(rising noon **dusk**)	(sunset twilight **dawn**)

18.	(**abundant** scattered loathsome)	(plentiful **scarce** loaded)
19.	(malevolent **brave** candid)	(courageous dastardly **cowardly**)
20.	(flexible **debilitated** worried)	(**strong** weak whining)
21.	(pantry basement **attic**)	(roof **cellar** porch)
22.	(reverence **despair** faith)	(**hope** misery desolation)
23.	(scaffold **build** structure)	(stack create **destroy**)
24.	(**humble** whisper wicked)	(modest **proud** enslaved)
25.	(aghast **ajar** afar)	(open peak **closed**)
26.	(**sow** seed water)	(plant **reap** cow)
27.	(net sheer **opaque**)	(blocked translucent **transparent**)
28.	(**vacant** conspicuous rent)	(spacious **occupied** empty)
29.	(excellence fight **virtue**)	(**vice** victory good)
30.	(**wax** clean wick)	(increase candle **wane**)

Billy's Puzzle Page: Find the antonym apples (page 17)

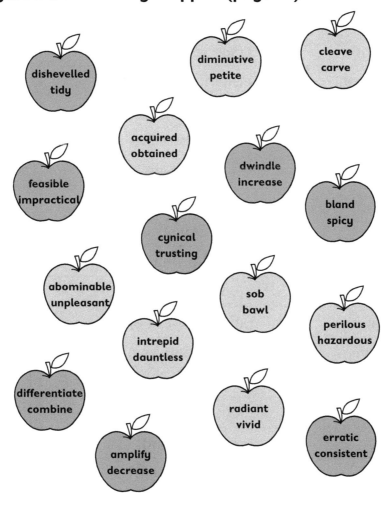

Lesson 3 answers: Create a Compound Word

Develop: Create a Compound Word (page 19)

1.	(all **day** over)	(brake bored **break**)
2.	(**book** queen sink)	(king **let** token)
3.	(earn good **clock**)	(**wise** nest news)
4.	(same **be** by)	(**came** ten hive)
5.	(at up **back**)	(lass **fire** stares)
6.	(**air** at a)	(**line** whole plain)
7.	(doll **cup** flaw)	(**board** saucer led)
8.	(**brain** vie great)	(tall **stem** surgery)
9.	(for **fore** deep)	(sea sore **cast**)
10.	(**hedge** war all)	(**hog** maze most)

Succeed: Create a Compound Word (pages 20–21)

1.	(**for** in some)	(**get** hand front)
2.	(wreck **copy** fast)	(less **right** break)
3.	(see tree **grand**)	(**son** more acre)
4.	(**card** cross stone)	(shark did **board**)
5.	(dead pierce **head**)	(end **ache** ear)
6.	(care **ear** in)	(**ring** case rake)
7.	(**for** plaster more)	(**bid** cast head)
8.	(**book** sink queen)	(**case** king cover)
9.	(for **jig** good)	(see **saw** band)
10.	(black pencil **key**)	(**stroke** whole bored)
11.	(all **mean** new)	(**while** girl agent)
12.	(**life** sure ladies)	(timed foot **like**)
13.	(four **pay** reign)	(boots **day** saw)
14.	(**new** by in)	(**found** print view)
15.	(tooth head **set**)	(out **back** led)
16.	(many **six** my)	(**fold** tie team)
17.	(back son **to**)	(knight **day** let)
18.	(**under** sweet over)	(**current** wait where)

19.	(four **tar** so)	(row **get** die)
20.	(sport hare **table**)	(wear trick **cloth**)
21.	(slow **up** no)	(**beat** stares write)
22.	(in cell **under**)	(**garment** over thyme)
23.	(**wash** hang stir)	(up shin **stand**)
24.	(sun **tea** cheque)	(glass mate **pot**)
25.	(**super** bitter be)	(suite **impose** hive)
26.	(new bake **pay**)	(**roll** in where)
27.	(food **waist** wedding)	(**band** truck bin)
28.	(gym **free** time)	(bag stop **style**)
29.	(**up** over back)	(**thrust** stares route)
30.	(**with** drawer bake)	(fall **out** inn)

Billy's Puzzle Page: ABC compound words (page 22)

Here are some example answers (other answers are possible):

A	along	+	side	=	alongside
B	back	+	stroke	=	backstroke
C	counter	+	clockwise	=	counterclockwise
D	day	+	light	=	daylight
E	earth	+	worm	=	earthworm
F	fire	+	flies	=	fireflies
G	good	+	night	=	goodnight
H	hand	+	cuff	=	handcuff
I	in	+	fuse	=	infuse
J	jelly	+	fish	=	jellyfish
K	key	+	board	=	keyboard
L	law	+	suit	=	lawsuit
M	moon	+	walk	=	moonwalk
N	nut	+	cracker	=	nutcracker
O	over	+	coat	=	overcoat
P	play	+	ground	=	playground
Q	quick	+	sand	=	quicksand
R	rain	+	fall	=	rainfall
S	ship	+	yard	=	shipyard

T	team	+	work	=	teamwork
U	under	+	arm	=	underarm
V	volley	+	ball	=	volleyball
W	watch	+	dog	=	watchdog
X	*There are no compound words that begin with the letter x.*				
Y	your	+	self	=	yourself
Z	zoo	+	keeper	=	zookeeper

Lesson 4 answers: Find the Missing Letter

Develop: Find the Missing Letter (page 24)

I.	sa (w) ind	ho (w) ho
2.	min (d) are	san (d) art
3.	scar (e) at	fre (e) el
4.	wors (t) rain	ju (t) ear
5.	boo (k) eep	ran (k) ing
6.	sk (y) ield	war (y) ours
7.	dic (e) nd	lac (e) arn
8.	lea (f) ry	scar (f) rail
9.	hu (g) rind	youn (g) naw
10.	crow (n) appy	know (n) ovel

Succeed: Find the Missing Letter (pages 25–26)

I.	churc (h) ate	scorc (h) eed
2.	bod (e) very	lam (e) agre
3.	close (t) able	tar (t) here
4.	clea (n) eat	bor (n) iece
5.	hoo (d) eal	men (d) ry
6.	bar (b) ruise	absor (b) elt
7.	car (p) rey	slur (p) orch
8.	war (m) ould	wor (m) ice
9.	wol (f) ind	tur (f) ield
10.	car (p) rince	usur (p) ride

11.	hu (g) one	lun (g) ame
12.	ar (m) edal	swar (m) ight
13.	reac (h) eart	sig (h) ear
14.	ree (k) not	wea (k) nee
15.	kil (n) ight	tur (n) ewt
16.	fea (r) ead	fo (r) ind
17.	meta (l) ow	hal (l) east
18.	los (s) erve	his (s) in
19.	clas (s) low	ha (s) earch
20.	car (t) orn	ten (t) ime
21.	fo (g) rid	co (g) rief
22.	chor (e) ast	sal (e) bb
23.	so (w) ed	endo (w) ield
24.	fir (m) ate	alar (m) eal
25.	sa (g) oat	son (g) rade
26.	pla (y) ield	pa (y) ear
27.	plan (t) reat	star (t) ight
28.	tom (b) uy	lam (b) ury
29.	stra (w) orry	blo (w) eary
30.	faw (n) ext	scor (n) ine

Billy's Puzzle Page: Word snakes (page 27)

Here are some example answers (other answers are possible):

1. sig (n) ew (t) urre (t) ea (m) ilk

2. eg (g) rat (e) art (h) ur (t) ake

3. nai (l) ear (n) ex (t) ende (r) oots

4. foo (t) eacu (p) on (d) rai (n) ever

5. wreat (h) un (t) ea (r) unne (r) ail

Lesson 5 answers: Move a Letter

Develop: Move a Letter (page 29)

1.	blend	tale	b = lend table
2.	paint	host	i = pant hoist
3.	peace	car	e = pace care
4.	scare	bled	e = scar bleed
5.	planet	each	t = plane teach
6.	swing	here	w = sing where
7.	forge	rein	g = fore reign
8.	hover	eats	h = over heats
9.	estate	clan	e = state clean
10.	left	oil	f = let foil

Succeed: Move a Letter (pages 30–31)

1.	beacon	vent	e = bacon event
2.	voice	her	o = vice hero
3.	threat	tanks	h = treat thanks
4.	witch	hair	c = with chair
5.	mince	ear	n = mice near /earn
6.	munch	pat	n = much pant
7.	driver	tout	r = drive /diver trout
8.	teamed	appal	e = tamed appeal
9.	done	well	d = one dwell
10.	board	ice	d = boar dice
11.	spine	and	s = pine sand
12.	stage	poser	t = sage poster
13.	three	trust	h = tree thrust
14.	gasped	boater	s = gaped boaster /boaters
15.	twine	crate	e = twin create
16.	thrust	sake	h = trust shake
17.	bear	link	b = ear blink
18.	filled	party	l = filed partly

19.	hooped	shut	o = hoped shout
20.	bread	root	b = read robot
21.	latches	with	c = lathes witch
22.	carer	bake	r = care baker /brake
23.	block	rain	b = lock brain
24.	leaden	father	e = laden feather
25.	greed	son	g = reed song
26.	mister	sand	t = miser stand
27.	pitch	hath	c = pith hatch
28.	string	camp	r = sting cramp
29.	barged	stager	g = bared stagger
30.	movie	host	i = move hoist

Billy's Puzzle Page: Word ladders (page 32)

Here are some example answers:

S E A T	**C A R E**	**H A N D**
B E A T	C A M E	L A N D
B O A T	C A M P	L E N D
B O L T	L A M P	L E A D
B O L D	**L I M P**	**L E A F**

C O M B	**R O S E**	**L I M B**
C O M E	R I S E	L I M E
C O P E	R I P E	L I N E
H O P E	R I P S	L A N E
H Y P E	**T I P S**	**M A N E**

Lesson 6 answers: Find the Missing Three-Letter Word

Develop: Find the Missing Three-Letter Word (page 34)

1.	RIB	I took some medicine for my **TERRIBLE** headache.
2.	POT	We **SPOTTED** elephants on the safari.
3.	PIT	I need to remember to use **CAPITAL** letters when I write.
4.	ANT	The inventor had developed a **FANTASTIC** idea.

5.	CUP	I reached for a mug out of the **CUPBOARD**.
6.	LOW	Mum received a beautiful bouquet of **FLOWERS**.
7.	TEN	I scanned the **CONTENTS** page for the chapter that I wanted.
8.	LEG	After the summer, the boy would attend **COLLEGE**.
9.	DEN	My uncle was in a car **ACCIDENT** and broke his leg.
10.	OWL	Dad was **SCOWLING** when I was late to meet him.

Succeed: Find the Missing Three-Letter Word (pages 35–36)

1.	ART	The race would **START** when we heard the whistle.
2.	LED	She demonstrated her **KNOWLEDGE** of computers.
3.	HER	Everyone **GATHERED** after the funeral.
4.	ACT	My grandfather **MANUFACTURES** toy cars.
5.	CON	The curry contained **COCONUT** milk.
6.	GOT	I had **FORGOTTEN** my lines in the school performance.
7.	BUS	The man's baking **BUSINESS** was a roaring success.
8.	ROT	**CARROT** cake is usually topped with cream cheese frosting.
9.	COP	The skyscraper had a **HELICOPTER** pad on the roof.
10.	CAP	The girl was more than **CAPABLE** of completing her homework independently.
11.	ROW	The bride still needed something **BORROWED** for the ceremony.
12.	AGE	The **VOYAGE** took longer than the sailor had anticipated.
13.	END	Hercules was a **LEGENDARY** warrior.
14.	LAW	The animal kept **CLAWING** at its cage.
15.	DEN	The ground had **HARDENED** because it hadn't rained for so long.
16.	INK	The chef would **SPRINKLE** salt and pepper on the food before sending it out.
17.	EAR	My nan wore a **HEARING** aid as she got older.
18.	ASH	He **WASHED** the potatoes before he peeled them.
19.	MEN	Finishing first was a **TREMENDOUS** result for the new driver.
20.	END	The children **PRETENDED** to be pirates in the garden.
21.	RUM	My dad makes a **SCRUMPTIOUS** lamb kleftiko.
22.	PEN	A **PENTAGON** is a five-sided shape.
23.	ATE	The witness **ACCURATELY** described the robber to the police.

24.	ATE	The teacher became **IRRITATED** when I didn't hand in my homework on time.
25.	ROB	My head **THROBBED** after I banged it.
26.	AND	The priest lit a **CANDLE** to begin the service.
27.	CAP	The thief artfully **ESCAPED** his prison cell.
28.	THE	The **AMPHITHEATRE** was filled with people.
29.	FAR	He bid his friend **FAREWELL** and he set off on a new adventure.
30.	BID	It was **FORBIDDEN** to enter the forest after dark.

Billy's Puzzle Page: Three-letter challenge (page 37)

Many different answers are possible.

Lesson 7 answers: Complete the Third Pair the Same Way

Develop: Complete the Third Pair the Same Way (page 40)

1.	pipe pip	mane man	song son *(drop the final letter)*
2.	hind hand	time tame	wisp wasp *(change the 'i' to an 'a')*
3.	beard ear	hoard oar	tales ale *(drop the first and last letter)*
4.	shout shot	solder sole	fluted flue *(number code 1235)*
5.	mammoth ham	million nil	matador rat *(number code 723)*
6.	emit time	keep peek	rats star *(mirrored words)*
7.	teams seam	fails sail	lands sand *(number code 5234)*
8.	bloat coat	cling ding	shout tout *(move the first letter one place along the alphabet and remove the second letter)*
9.	start tart	tripe ripe	place lace *(drop the first letter)*
10.	hinder rind	rented dent	parted dart *(number code 6234)*

Succeed: Complete the Third Pair the Same Way (pages 41–42)

1.	cabbages sage	wandered dare	focussed dose *(number code 8267)*
2.	define find	posted step	mother them *(number code 3451)*
3.	marks arm	ready ear	glove log *(number code 231)*
4.	flood good	boast cast	stale tale *(change the first letter to the next one in the alphabet and remove the second letter)*
5.	bread read	grain rain	cloud loud *(drop the first letter)*

6.	poster rest	wanted dent	hasten nest (number code 6534)
7.	bigot big	bushy bus	singe sin (drop the fourth and fifth letters)
8.	extent ten	places ape	inform fir (number code 315)
9.	many any	land and	said aid (drop the first letter)
10.	camera mace	sentry nest	casket sack (number code 3214)
11.	knits stink	spots stops	warts straw (mirrored words)
12.	grown row	bodes ode	brawl raw (drop the first and last letter)
13.	extending nets	attests sets	unsold loss (number code 543 and add s)
14.	mint tin	bows sow	hips sip (number code 423)
15.	mail nail	sale tale	bows cows (move the first letter one place along the alphabet)
16.	crash dash	flash gash	shape tape (move the first letter one place along the alphabet and drop the second letter)
17.	writer rite	shandy hand	tables able (drop the first and last letter)
18.	barmy bar	alert ale	cared car (drop the last two letters)
19.	fact act	sink ink	tout out (drop the first letter)
20.	ten net	war raw	saw was (mirrored words)
21.	ash sash	lit slit	lop slop (add an 's' to the front of the word)
22.	jump lump	dire fire	rail tail (move the first letter two places along the alphabet)
23.	live evil	star rats	time emit (mirrored words)
24.	fabric cab	jetsam met	caters sat (number code 623)
25.	all ball	ore pore	ear fear (move the first letter one place along the alphabet and add that letter to the front of the word)
26.	task ask	sand and	shop hop (drop the first letter)
27.	mobile lob	barber ear	ration oat (number code 523)
28.	grind grid	tramp trap	beard bead (remove the fourth letter)
29.	bile bite	male mate	vole vote (change the 'l' to a 't')
30.	custard card	violent vent	sailing sing (number code 1567)

Billy's Puzzle Page: Words within a word (page 43)

Many different answers are possible.

Lesson 8 answers: Create Words in the Same Way

Develop: Create Words in the Same Way (page 45)

1.	host (stir) iron	push (shin) inch
2.	path (have) veto	fall (lash) ship
3.	ban (and) day	gin (inn) new
4.	grass (asset) teach	known (owner) ready
5.	twin (want) tape	thus (host) tone
6.	rip (tip) fat	rug (bug) tub
7.	keep (deep) wild	cold (fold) wolf
8.	oak (oar) rim	fog (for) raw
9.	tech (cast) fast	rent (nice) dice
10.	rush (rust) talk	sale (salt) team

Succeed: Create Words in the Same Way (pages 46–47)

1.	virus (rusty) unity	thank (ankle) uncle
2.	cycle (clear) arena	shown (owner) error
3.	mate (tip) chip	duck (cat) flat
4.	hop (open) end	ego (gone) new
5.	sort (tray) yard	whom (moon) note
6.	bin (tin) yet	bad (sad) gas
7.	cost (stop) open	bath (thaw) away
8.	nets (sent) time	need (dens) soup
9.	live (even) seen	reef (fell) sell
10.	jar (art) top	won (one) ear
11.	goal (gold) glad	fray (free) were
12.	bribe (beats) stand	flesh (shirt) trips
13.	led (den) net	mug (gun) now
14.	sap (ape) end	ore (red) die
15.	train (trip) ripe	speak (spin) wine
16.	rice (rich) itch	pink (pick) lick
17.	hurt (turn) none	news (sewn) nice
18.	fluid (fluff) stuff	grade (grand) stand

19.	alarm (armed) delay	chair (aired) debut
20.	fate (test) stay	wife (fear) army
21.	young (youth) mouth	craft (crash) trash
22.	mail (like) knee	view (were) rose
23.	bond (boss) miss	life (link) sank
24.	leer (rein) pain	rush (husk) risk
25.	heart (earth) hence	plate (later) rough
26.	sag (age) egg	fax (axe) era
27.	treat (react) class	other (their) image
28.	moon (mode) debt	cook (come) mere
29.	mile (mill) lime	case (cask) kept
30.	lease (least) meant	sharp (share) solve

Billy's Puzzle Page: Word worms (page 48)

BEAD	BEAK	PEAK	PEAR	HEAR	BEAR	BEAN

MEAT	MEET	FEET	FEED	REED	READ	REAR

TRAM	CRAM	CLAM	CLAY	PRAY	TRAY	TRAP

Lesson 9 answers: Find the Hidden Four-Letter Word

Develop: Find the Hidden Four-Letter Word (page 50)

1.	Each alligator was fed a bucket of fish a day.	HALL
2.	The new boy ate by himself at lunch.	THEN
3.	The storm ended by morning.	MEND
4.	My aunt finally sold her car today.	CART
5.	The first arrow found the target.	STAR
6.	He fell over and scraped his knee.	LOVE
7.	I couldn't see the television from this angle.	SANG
8.	That wind is bracing.	TWIN
9.	My sister bought her new top at the store.	NEWT
10.	The attack caught them by surprise.	HEAT

Succeed: Find the Hidden Four-Letter Word (pages 51–52)

1.	The rooster crowed at dawn.	HERO
2.	Sam also loved music.	SOLO
3.	There was a lot of risk in this plan.	SKIN
4.	My stomach felt sore inside.	REIN
5.	An apple costs thirty pence.	TYPE
6.	The cleaners entered the hotel suite.	SENT
7.	Recycling plastic can help our planet.	POUR
8.	The little boys hoped for snow.	SHOP
9.	It was the worst open day he had been to.	STOP
10.	His other daughters were jealous.	HERD
11.	Nemo damaged his fin during his escape.	FIND
12.	The fierce enemy thought they had won.	MYTH
13.	A seamstress altered my wedding dress.	SALT
14.	The police were very confused.	EVER
15.	His team scored the most points in the league.	THEM
16.	These alleys lead out of the town.	SEAL
17.	She called out the register.	HERE
18.	The wren travelled to the closest branch.	RENT
19.	Five invites were delivered by post.	VEIN
20.	I couldn't wait for my birthday party.	FORM
21.	The baby grew rapidly in his first few months.	WRAP
22.	It was spring one day and suddenly it was summer.	GONE
23.	Appearing in the water was a long ripple.	GRIP
24.	Time always flies when you are having fun.	MEAL
25.	Mum made them eat their vegetables.	MEAT
26.	The woman was granted a completely new identity.	WIDE
27.	Dinner consisted of mash and sausages.	HAND
28.	The careless young lad left behind his homework.	GLAD
29.	The competitive athlete had a sudden thirst.	DENT
30.	The photographer took the picture quickly.	EPIC

Billy's Puzzle Page: Spell the four-letter words (page 53)

Many different answers are possible. For example:

First triangle: RANT, TAIL

Second triangle: LATE, ATOM

Third triangle: COIN, CAST

Lesson 10 answers: Anagram Sentences

Develop: Anagram Sentences (page 55)

1.	A	I prefer to **READ** a book rather than **WATCH** television.
2.	A	We **DANCED** underneath the Moon **THAT** night.
3.	R	The **FLOWERS** grew despite the heavy **RAIN**.
4.	E	I have to **WEAR** my PE kit on **TUESDAYS**.
5.	T	In the **TOWER**, a princess **SLEPT**.
6.	A	You **HAVE** to boil water to **MAKE** tea.
7.	T	A **LOT** of people **BOUGHT** tickets for the concert.
8.	O	I **WOULD** choose salted popcorn **OVER** sweet.
9.	A	The sign **SAID STAY** off the grass.
10.	A	I never **PLAY** football after **DARK**.

Succeed: Anagram Sentences (pages 56–57)

1.	U	I wore my wellies to **JUMP** in muddy **PUDDLES**.
2.	F	We have **FISH** and chips on **FRIDAYS** at school.
3.	I	My **FAVOURITE** flavour of **CRISPS** is cheese and onion.
4.	S	**SUNCREAM** protects your **SKIN** from the sun.
5.	E	I watch the **NEWS** whilst **EATING** my breakfast.
6.	O	The **HOMEMADE** lemonade was extremely **SOUR**.
7.	I	I braided my **HAIR** before **GOING** to bed.
8.	T	We **BUILT** a snowman with a **CARROT** for a nose.
9.	A	The ice-cream **BEGAN** to melt because of the **HEAT**.
10.	N	Four ducklings were **FOUND** inside their **NEST**.
11.	E	A burglar was **ARRESTED** for breaking and **ENTERING**.
12.	O	Apples fell **FROM** the trees in the **ORCHARD**.

13.	L	I was **LATE** for **SCHOOL** so I had to get the bus.
14.	K	My car **BROKE** down on the way to **WORK**.
15.	I	Rapunzel let down her **HAIR** for the prince to **CLIM**B.
16.	G	The **TIGER** paced restlessly in its **CAGE** at the zoo.
17.	B	We went ten-pin **BOWLING** for my **BIRTHDAY**.
18.	E	The teacher expected the **HOMEWORK** to be handed in on **TIME**.
19.	P	A genie **APPEARED** when the **LAMP** was rubbed.
20.	E	**OUTSIDE** the palace was a beautiful **GARDEN**.
21.	E	There was a **PEA** underneath the princess's **BED**.
22.	T	The geese were flying **SOUTH** for the **WINTER**.
23.	R	The television **BLARED** from the other **ROOM**.
24.	I	"**PICK** up your toys before dinner," Dad **SAID**.
25.	N	Santa knows whether you have been **NAUGHTY** or **NICE**.
26.	S	Spotlights **SHONE** down upon the actor on the **STAGE**.
27.	D	The **DELIVERY** man left the parcel by the **DOOR**.
28.	N	I bought **NEW** glasses after visiting the **OPTICIAN**.
29.	E	The doctor **PRESCRIBED** me some medicine for my **ILLNESS**.
30.	I	**FIREWORKS** lit up the sky on Bonfire **NIGHT**.

Billy's Puzzle Page: Anagrams (page 58)

HORSE	HEART	BREAD
SHORE	**EARTH**	**BEARD**
SMILE	PLATE	CRATE
SLIME	**PETAL**	**TRACE**

Here are some example answers:

S T A T E   **T A S T E**

T H E R E   **T H R E E**

W E I R D   **W I R E D**

Lesson 11 answers: Solve Letter Sums

Develop: Solve Letter Sums (page 61)

1.	B	$15 - 10 = 5$
2.	B	$12 + 18 \div 3 = 18$
3.	E	$36 \div 9 = 4$
4.	B	$24 \div 8 = 3$
5.	C	$35 \div 7 = 5$
6.	B	$4 + 6 = 10$
7.	E	$30 - 18 = 12$
8.	C	$16 + 9 = 25, C^2 = 25, C = 5$
9.	C	$30 \div 5 = 6$
10.	C	$32 - 12 = 20$

Succeed: Solve Letter Sums (pages 62–63)

1.	A	$28 - 3 = 25$
2.	D	$6 \times 9 = 54$
3.	B	$80 + 4 = 84$
4.	A	$38 + 12 = 50$
5.	E	$75 - 50 = 25$
6.	D	$5 \times 8 = 40$
7.	E	$16 - 4 = 12$
8.	B	$30 - 6 = 24$
9.	B	$25 - 5 = 20$
10.	B	$3 \times 12 = 36$
11.	D	$45 - 10 = 35$
12.	D	$12 + 10 = 22$
13.	A	$4 \times 7 = 28$
14.	E	$100 \div 5 = 20$
15.	B	$7 \times 7 = 49$
16.	D	$22 + 28 = 50$
17.	C	$10 + 3 = 13$
18.	C	$72 \div 8 = 9$

19.	D	$48 \div 12 = 4$ $4 - 2 = 2$
20.	D	$36 \div 6 = 6$
21.	C	$60 \div 12 = 5$
22.	B	$110 - 30 = 80$
23.	A	$8 \times 9 = 72$
24.	D	$36 - 6 = 30$
25.	D	$4 + 16 = 20$
26.	E	$3 + 45 = 48$
27.	C	$25 \div 5 = 5$
28.	C	$32 \div 4 = 8$
29.	D	$40 - 9 = 31$
30.	B	$24 + 16 = 40$

Billy's Puzzle Page: Expensive letters (page 64)

Here is an example of a word that costs exactly 50p:

A P P L E

$1 + 16 + 16 + 12 + 5 = 50$

Lesson 12 answers: Continue the Number Series

Develop: Continue the Number Series (page 66)

1.	15	Halve the previous number
2.	29	+6
3.	24	+1, +2, +3, etc.
4.	15	Alternate pattern: +2, −2, +2, −2
5.	96	Double the previous number
6.	49	Ascending square numbers
7.	86	+5, +10, +15, +20, etc.
8.	45	−8
9.	69	−1, −2, −3, etc.
10.	36	Alternate pattern: −3, +5, −3, +5

Succeed: Continue the Number Series (pages 67–68)

1.	42	+2
2.	12	Alternate pattern: +3, +5, +3, +5
3.	72	9 × table
4.	25	Descending square numbers
5.	43	−7
6.	19	Alternate pattern: +5, −2, +5, −2
7.	51	Alternate pattern: −1, −1, −1, −1
8.	125	Halve the previous number
9.	10	Alternate pattern: +2, +1, +2, +1
10.	8	Fibonacci sequence: add the two previous numbers
11.	256	Double the previous number
12.	72	+3, +6, +9, +12, etc.
13.	47	Add the two previous numbers (Fibonacci sequence)
14.	14	−1, +2, −2, +3, −3, etc.
15.	200	Halve the previous number
16.	224	Double the previous number
17.	65	Alternate pattern: −7, +1, −7, +1
18.	74	+9, +11, +13, +15, etc.
19.	9	Alternate pattern: +4, −2, +4, −2
20.	243	Multiply the previous number by 3
21.	78	+13
22.	58	Alternate pattern: the difference between the odd terms is −5, −10, −15, etc.
23.	232	−40
24.	16	Divide the previous number by 2
25.	124	+1, +3, +5, +7, +9, etc.
26.	21	+1, +2, +3, +4, etc.
27.	27	−2, −4, −6, −8, −10
28.	192	×1, ×2, ×3, ×4, etc.
29.	16	Alternate descending square numbers
30.	486	×3

Billy's Puzzle Page: Matching game (page 69)

5 10 15 20	Add 0.5
27 24 21 18	Subtract 9
2 4 8 16	Add 5
1000 100 10 1	Multiply by 2
24 36 48 60	Subtract 3
81 72 63 54	Add 12
2 6 18 54	Divide by 10
100 50 25	Multiply by 3
1 1.5 2 2.5	Divide by 2

Lesson 13 answers: Find the Number to Complete the Sum

Develop: Find the Number to Complete the Sum (page 72)	
1.	2
2.	3
3.	4
4.	14
5.	6
6.	3
7.	8
8.	2
9.	6
10.	29

Succeed: Find the Number to Complete the Sum (pages 73–74)			
1.	10	11.	156
2.	2	12.	409
3.	15	13.	592
4.	5	14.	94
5.	12	15.	628
6.	3	16.	1554
7.	2	17.	771
8.	7	18.	1067
9.	6	19.	1005
10.	5	20.	560

Billy's Puzzle Page: Beat the clock! (page 75)

Answers will depend on the numbers chosen.

Lesson 14 answers: Find the Missing Number

Develop: Find the Missing Number (page 77)

1.	45	Add together
2.	54	Subtract
3.	8	Divide
4.	32	Multiply
5.	24	Add 1 to the first number and multiply by the last number
6.	22	Multiply then divide by 4
7.	12	Find the square roots and add the numbers together
8.	7	Divide
9.	17	Subtract the numbers from each other and halve
10.	62	Add the numbers together and multiply by 2

Succeed: Find the Missing Number (pages 78–79)

1.	11	Divide the third number by the first number
2.	49	Multiply then add 1
3.	69	Subtract
4.	52	Add
5.	34	Multiply
6.	12	Divide
7.	26	Find the midpoint
8.	64	Halve the third number and multiply by the first number
9.	40	Double the third number and add the numbers together
10.	84	Add
11.	11	Divide
12.	75	Square each number and then subtract the smaller number from the larger one
13.	63	Multiply
14.	47	Double the third number and subtract it from the first number
15.	28	Subtract
16.	145	Square each number and then add the numbers together

17.	46	Halve the numbers and then add them together
18.	35	Find the midpoint
19.	51	Multiply
20.	137	Add
21.	34	Add, divide by 2 and add 1
22.	13	Divide
23.	46	Subtract
24.	14	Add, divide by 4 and subtract 1
25.	66	Add then double
26.	84	Multiply
27.	13	Divide
28.	72	Double the third number and then add the numbers together
29.	157	Add
30.	29	Subtract

Billy's Puzzle Page: Find the missing number (page 80)

Answer: 16

Solution: Subtract the smaller external number from the larger one. Multiply the answer by 2. Then square it.

$9 - 7 = 2$

$2 \times 2 = 4$

$4^2 = 16$

Lesson 15 answers: Crack the Letter Code

Develop: Crack the Letter Code (page 84)

1.	MATHS	Pattern: +1
2.	RESPOND	Pattern: −1, −2, −3…
3.	DARK	Pattern: +2
4.	TXQBO	Pattern: −3
5.	FIZQY	Pattern: +5
6.	MLEVO	Mirror code

7.	SZGV	Mirror code
8.	GLDM	Mirror code
9.	PLAY	Mirror code
10.	WINDOW	Mirror code

Succeed: Crack the Letter Code (pages 85–86)

1.	DIRGV	Mirror code
2.	TRIO	Mirror code
3.	EMOANN	Pattern: −1, −2, −3…
4.	RSQV	Pattern: +2, +4, +2, +4…
5.	TEA	Pattern: +1
6.	SNEEZE	Pattern: +1, +2, +3
7.	JUMP	Mirror code
8.	SHORTS	Mirror code
9.	ZDZPV	Mirror code
10.	IZRM	Mirror code
11.	GIZRM	Mirror code
12.	BPCYK	Pattern: −2
13.	UDTS	Pattern: +1, −1, +1, −1…
14.	HQG	Pattern: +3, +3 +3
15.	CINEMA	Mirror code
16.	SISTER	Mirror code
17.	FOE	Mirror code
18.	SOCK	Pattern: −1
19.	CHIPS	Pattern: +5
20.	BLUE	Pattern: −2

Billy's Puzzle Page: Coded wordsearch (page 87)

Pattern: +1, +2, +3, etc.

HCPI	DQGI	BNSLFHLB	MGWXJXZ	TGDVHN
XQUH	GWQ	XKQ	MQVI	DTDGP

G	T	G	H	P	G	G	I	X	G	M	X	Q	K
L	Q	X	G	V	S	F	M	K	X	W	Z	D	G
K	T	T	G	S	C	G	G	Q	X	G	D	I	G
I	N	T	I	H	V	L	W	X	K	T	X	G	V
L	X	S	M	N	H	V	D	G	T	C	D	Q	N
M	P	P	M	G	S	N	B	B	V	I	H	D	Q
X	M	K	B	N	S	L	F	H	L	B	I	L	Z
C	Q	Q	C	I	F	Z	X	J	X	W	G	M	B
D	Y	V	J	P	Z	B	B	W	L	H	H	J	I
M	I	Z	D	G	H	Q	B	M	I	U	P	W	G
V	D	W	W	D	D	H	Q	U	H	Q	W	W	J
G	X	X	W	T	I	Q	Q	W	T	X	W	F	H
W	Z	M	L	D	H	I	G	X	H	D	F	T	D
Q	G	I	Q	L	V	S	V	J	D	U	I	G	Q

Lesson 16 answers: Crack the Number Code

Develop: Crack the Number Code (page 90)

1.	4296
2.	9231
3.	WAND
4.	6721
5.	5668

6.	FATE
7.	7463
8.	8166
9.	GALA

Succeed: Crack the Number Code (pages 91–92)

1.	6523		12.	CAST
2.	3529		13.	8465
3.	RUNG		14.	8442
4.	6042		15.	ALLY
5.	6420		16.	9123
6.	LAME		17.	1636
7.	9511		18.	TOSS
8.	6539		19.	7412
9.	SKIM		20.	7251
10.	3146		21.	DEED
11.	6431			

Billy's Puzzle Page: Coded sums (page 93)

1.	8642 − 3090 = 5552
2.	9341 − 8720 = 621
3.	2469 + 5156 = 7625
4.	9365 + 9830 = 19,195
5.	8704 − 6821 = 1883
6.	4926 + 5905 = 10,831
7.	7013 − 3854 = 3159
8.	6459 + 3060 = 9519

Lesson 17 answers: Complete the Letter Series

Develop: Complete the Letter Series (page 95)

1.	PK	Mirror pairs +3
2.	JU	First letters: +1; second letters: +1 and repeat
3.	KW	First letters: +1, +2, +3, +4; second letters: −1
4.	PL	First letters: −1; second letters: +2
5.	RN	First letters: −2; second letters: +2
6.	VL	First letters: +5; second letters: −2; repeat
7.	GJ	First letters: +1; second letters: +2

8.	EV	Mirror pairs +1
9.	VQ	First letters: −1, −2, −3, −4; second letters: +1
10.	IJ	Alphabet pairs +2

Succeed: Complete the Letter Series (page 96)

1.	VM	First letters: −1; second letters: +1, +2, +1, +2
2.	KP	Mirror pairs +2
3.	PK	First letters: −3; second letters: +1; repeat
4.	UV	First letters: +2; second letters: +2
5.	HI	First letters: +2, −1, +2, −1; second letters: +2
6.	IK	First letters: +2; second letters: + 2
7.	NR	First letters: +1; second letters: +1, −1, +1, −1
8.	FS	First letters: +2; second letters: +1, +2, +3, +4
9.	RS	First letters: −2, −4, −2, −4; second letters: −1
10.	KP	Mirror pairs −3
11.	DI	First letters: −4; second letters: −2
12.	LV	First letters: −5, −4, −3, −2; second letters: −1, −3, −1, −3
13.	ER	First letters: +1; second letters: +2, −1, +2, −1
14.	BA	First letters: −1, −2, −3, −4; second letters: +1, +2, +3, +4
15.	LO	Mirror pairs +1, +2, +3, +4

Billy's Puzzle Page: Closest to 50 (page 97)

Answers will vary.

Lesson 18 answers: Complete the Letter Sentence

Develop: Complete the Letter Sentence (page 99)

1.	BP	First letter: −2; second letter: +2
2.	OF	First letter: +3; second letter: +3
3.	PX	First letter: −3; second letter: +1
4.	RJ	First letter: +2; second letter: +3
5.	HP	First letter: +1; second letter: −4
6.	XX	First letter: −5; second letter: +1

7.	AQ	First letter: +1; second letter: +2
8.	RK	First letter: −1; second letter: −2
9.	UA	First letter: +3; second letter: −3
10.	GA	First letter: +2; second letter: +1

Succeed: Complete the Letter Sentence (page 100)

1.	AV	First letter: −1; second letter: +6
2.	EJ	First letter: −2; second letter: −2
3.	MZ	First letter: −3; second letter: +2
4.	FI	First letter: +2; second letter: −4
5.	XD	First letter: −1; second letter: +1
6.	ZE	First letter: −3; second letter: +3
7.	EQ	First letter: −5; second letter: +2
8.	XG	First letter: −3; second letter: +2
9.	IH	First letter: −4; second letter: +2
10.	MT	First letter: −3; second letter: +3
11.	JZ	First letter: +4; second letter: −3
12.	CP	First letter: +1; second letter: −2
13.	XU	First letter: +5; second letter: −5
14.	EZ	First letter: −2; second letter: +3
15.	HY	First letter: −3; second letter: +1

Billy's Puzzle Page: Alphabet race (page 101)

Answers will vary.

Marking Chart

Fill in the tables below with your results from each of the Succeed timed tests.

Lesson 1: Closest in Meaning	/30		**Lesson 10:** Anagram Sentences	/30
Lesson 2: Opposite in Meaning	/30		**Lesson 11:** Solve Letter Sums	/30
Lesson 3: Create a Compound Word	/30		**Lesson 12:** Continue the Number Series	/30
Lesson 4: Find the Missing Letter	/30		**Lesson 13:** Find the Number to Complete the Sum	/20
Lesson 5: Move a Letter	/30		**Lesson 14:** Find the Missing Number	/30
Lesson 6: Find the Missing Three-Letter Word	/30		**Lesson 15:** Crack the Letter Code	/20
Lesson 7: Complete the Third Pair the Same Way	/30		**Lesson 16:** Crack the Number Code	/21
Lesson 8: Create Words in the Same Way	/30		**Lesson 17:** Complete the Letter Series	/15
Lesson 9: Find the Hidden Four-Letter Word	/30		**Lesson 18:** Complete the Letter Sentence	/15
Total Score				/481

WELL DONE!

Progress Grid

Colour these charts with your score from each Succeed test to see how well you have done.

Lesson 1: Closest in Meaning

1	2	3	4	5	6	7	8	9	10	11	12	13	14	15	16	17	18	19	20	21	22	23	24	25	26	27	28	29	30

Lesson 2: Opposite in Meaning

1	2	3	4	5	6	7	8	9	10	11	12	13	14	15	16	17	18	19	20	21	22	23	24	25	26	27	28	29	30

Lesson 3: Create a Compound Word

1	2	3	4	5	6	7	8	9	10	11	12	13	14	15	16	17	18	19	20	21	22	23	24	25	26	27	28	29	30

Lesson 4: Find the Missing Letter

1	2	3	4	5	6	7	8	9	10	11	12	13	14	15	16	17	18	19	20	21	22	23	24	25	26	27	28	29	30

Lesson 5: Move a Letter

1	2	3	4	5	6	7	8	9	10	11	12	13	14	15	16	17	18	19	20	21	22	23	24	25	26	27	28	29	30

Lesson 6: Find the Missing Three-Letter Word

1	2	3	4	5	6	7	8	9	10	11	12	13	14	15	16	17	18	19	20	21	22	23	24	25	26	27	28	29	30

Lesson 7: Complete the Third Pair the Same Way

1	2	3	4	5	6	7	8	9	10	11	12	13	14	15	16	17	18	19	20	21	22	23	24	25	26	27	28	29	30

Lesson 8: Create Words in the Same Way

1	2	3	4	5	6	7	8	9	10	11	12	13	14	15	16	17	18	19	20	21	22	23	24	25	26	27	28	29	30

Lesson 9: Find the Hidden Four-Letter Word

1	2	3	4	5	6	7	8	9	10	11	12	13	14	15	16	17	18	19	20	21	22	23	24	25	26	27	28	29	30

Read the statements below for some hints and tips.

Re-read the Learn section and have another go at the Develop questions.	Good effort! Have another go at the questions you got wrong.	Well done! Keep up the good work.

Lesson 10: Anagram Sentences

1	2	3	4	5	6	7	8	9	10	11	12	13	14	15	16	17	18	19	20	21	22	23	24	25	26	27	28	29	30

Lesson 11: Solve Letter Sums

1	2	3	4	5	6	7	8	9	10	11	12	13	14	15	16	17	18	19	20	21	22	23	24	25	26	27	28	29	30

Lesson 12: Continue the Number Series

1	2	3	4	5	6	7	8	9	10	11	12	13	14	15	16	17	18	19	20	21	22	23	24	25	26	27	28	29	30

Lesson 13: Find the Number to Complete the Sum

1	2	3	4	5	6	7	8	9	10	11	12	13	14	15	16	17	18	19	20

Lesson 14: Find the Missing Number

1	2	3	4	5	6	7	8	9	10	11	12	13	14	15	16	17	18	19	20	21	22	23	24	25	26	27	28	29	30

Lesson 15: Crack the Letter Code

1	2	3	4	5	6	7	8	9	10	11	12	13	14	15	16	17	18	19	20

Lesson 16: Crack the Number Code

1	2	3	4	5	6	7	8	9	10	11	12	13	14	15	16	17	18	19	20	21

Lesson 17: Complete the Letter Series

1	2	3	4	5	6	7	8	9	10	11	12	13	14	15

Lesson 18: Complete the Letter Sentence

1	2	3	4	5	6	7	8	9	10	11	12	13	14	15

Read the statements below for some hints and tips.

Re-read the Learn section and have another go at the Develop questions.	Good effort! Have another go at the questions you got wrong.	Well done! Keep up the good work.

Notes